Minutemen and Mariners

Also by Charles F. Haywood

NO SHIP MAY SAIL
YOU NEED A COMPLETE REST
EASTWARD THE SEA
YANKEE DICTIONARY

Minutemen and Mariners
TRUE TALES OF NEW ENGLAND

By Charles F. Haywood
ILLUSTRATED

DODD, MEAD & COMPANY   New York

To my wife Dorothy

Acknowledgments

I WISH TO ACKNOWLEDGE the assistance that I have received from the Essex Institute and the Peabody Museum, both of Salem, Massachusetts, the Lynn Public Library and its staff, the Public Library of Machias, Maine, and its very helpful librarian, and the Lynn Historical Society.

Also I wish to acknowledge the courtesy shown to me by United States Navy personnel when I was aboard the frigate *Constitution* at the Boston Naval Shipyard. The Navy's Office of Naval Records and Library has rendered great service to all who do research in the field of American history by publishing the *Naval Documents Related to the United States Wars with the Barbary Powers* in six volumes. For facts and for the atmosphere of that era, these volumes are of unique value.

Especially do I wish to express appreciation for the help given me by my wife, Dorothy C. Haywood, Chief Librarian of the Lynn Public Library. Not only did she assist in making available the resources of the unusual collection of books on early American history in her library but she worked with me throughout the writing of this book. Her advice as a librarian was invaluable.

Contents

Illustrations

Minutemen and Mariners

1

The O'Brien Navy

IN THE YEAR 1740 a young Irishman named Morris O'Brien
left Dublin and took ship for the New World, hoping to find
in America the opportunities lacking in his native land, then
firmly controlled by an English tyranny. He found America
to his liking and settled in Scarboro in the southern part of
what is now the state of Maine but was then the British
province of Massachusetts.

Even though Irishmen were restive under the rule of the
British tyrant, many of them made excellent soldiers for the
English King. Morris was one of these. He joined the British
expedition against the French fortress of Louisburg, fought
well and came home with the rest of the New England troops
when finally the English flag floated above the walls of this
place so often called the key to North America.

The American environment was good for Morris O'Brien.
He married, and as the years rolled by his wife presented him
with three handsome daughters and a platoon of six sons who
were the sort of boys this new land needed. Jeremiah, Gideon,
John, William, Dennis and Joseph would be heard from
later, he figured, as they daily grew in strength and capability.

1

In the early days of America a large family of children was
not a burden to the father; it was an asset. Today a parent
who has to find the money to pay for "necessities" and "opportunities" for nine children needs to have an excellent
salary or relatives willing to help. In Morris O'Brien's time
children were given duties to perform when they reached
the age where they could walk unassisted, and these tasks increased with each year, so that one with nine children had
a good labor battalion for any frontier project. That doubtless was the reason why, in 1760, he decided to move to
Machias, a place on the Maine coast far to the east of the
Penobscot and only a short distance from the Canadian
border.

This was in territory where but recently any settlers lived
under the dread shadow of raids by the French and the Indians; a land where any man, as he hacked out fields from
the dark surrounding forest, faced the possibility that by
sundown his scalp might be dangling from some redskin's
belt and his wife and children on their way to captivity in
some Indian or French stronghold up north. However, Machias in 1760 was safe, for the power of the French in America
had been broken and the Indians had drawn far back into
the forests. Settlers might work undisturbed at making homes
in the wilderness.

From Penobscot Bay to the St. Croix River in New Bruns-
wick, the little settlement at Machias was the only place
where any considerable number of white people lived. Here,
Morris O'Brien thought, lay opportunity for him and his
growing family. He was right; the O'Brien family prospered.
He built a sawmill, and the logs from the vast forests along
the Machias River were floated down to be worked into beams

and boards by the saws in his establishment.

So important was the O'Brien mill that the townsfolk called this locality "Dublin" as their compliment to this hardworking Irish family. Lumber always has an excellent market, particularly when it may be transported cheaply in ships. By schooners the O'Brien product was carried down the coast to the active and growing towns of Massachusetts, especially Salem and Boston. In the Massachusetts Bay region, well settled for over a hundred years, the forests had been cut down and farming country extended far inland, so lumber for the coastal cities had to come by a long journey over poor roads by ox team. Much cheaper in seaboard cities was ship-borne Maine lumber.

The years following 1760 were a time of prosperity and growth along the eastern shore of Maine and indeed in the whole North country, now that the dread menace of French and Indian raids was removed by the British victory on the Plains of Abraham. Quebec had fallen, and Canada now belonged to England. Settlers could move eastward along the shore of Maine; they could move up the Merrimac, up the Connecticut, expanding year by year into what had been extremely dangerous territory.

Yet in this time of prosperity and growth came a new problem: the tension between the colonists and the Parliament in London, which laid new taxes on America to help pay the great debts incurred to fight the French war. The American colonists were enraged by the new taxes. Everywhere the people protested, held meetings, thwarted tax collectors, perpetrated illegal acts such as the Boston Tea Party and committed assaults on the King's troops such as that which culminated in the so-called Boston Massacre.

Who had won these lands from the Frenchman and the Indian? In England the answer was that the regular troops of the King had won them, and the Royal Navy. In America the reply was that colonial regiments fighting at Louisburg and in the wilderness, colonists at hundreds of forest outposts and at farms in numberless clearings had made this country English at last. Risking their scalps and the lives of their families; gradually turning the unbroken forest into a land of farms; living through lonely and severe winters, sometimes without enough to eat; building roads, churches and schools, they had made this America with no help whatsoever from those who sat in London, safe and fat and rich.

Morris O'Brien and his family lived in a town where the people knew the sound of the stealthy Indian's whistle in the forest. They had turned to in defense of their homes; they had labored on their roads and the church, and they had helped bury the scalped dead.

The people of Machias were sure they knew who had borne the burden of the war. They had. And Morris O'Brien was sure they had. He himself had fought in the Louisburg campaign. Further than that, his childhood and youth had been spent in old Ireland, where the image of a grasping and oppressive British government had clearly formed. To any rebellious feeling of his fellow townsmen in Machias he added with all the fervor of his Irish nature. So it was that there were no stronger patriots than the clan O'Brien on all that rugged coast.

The nineteenth day of April 1775 came and went in Machias, Maine, just like any other day. At Lexington and Concord a great battle was fought that day between the British Redcoats and the American Minutemen. The casualties

were high. The British were defeated and driven back into
Boston, and the American army was born. The first gunfire
on Lexington Green early that morning a poet years later
described as "the shot heard round the world."

The poet was right, in a sense, and yet the news of that
shot was not heard that day in Machias, Maine, nor the next
day; in fact, not until weeks afterward. Time was different in
1775; a lot more of it was required to accomplish anything.
On the day of Pearl Harbor, no one went to bed without
knowing what had happened on an island halfway across the
Pacific. On the day of the Concord fight, people in some parts
of Massachusetts did not hear of it for weeks. However, it
may be added that when they did hear, they were in no degree
surprised.

The news came to Machias in this way. Captain Ichabod
Jones called at Salem in early May with a schooner loaded
with Machias lumber. Sailing with him was another Machias
lumber schooner. At Salem they heard a full account of the
battle. The family of Captain Jones and the family of Captain Hilton, who commanded the other vessel, were in Boston,
in distress, for Boston was besieged by the American forces.
Their lines were a tight ring around the city, and food was
scarce.

The British drove a hard bargain with Captain Jones before they allowed him to depart with his family and his
furniture. Lumber was needed in the besieged city to build
barracks for the soldiers and houses for officers; because of
the siege none could come in over the road. Nor would any
nearby seaport supply lumber if it were known it was to
build a shelter for the Redcoats. So the British Admiral
Graves let Jones and the other captain have their families

on the condition that they bring two cargoes of lumber down from Machias to Boston for the construction of the barracks.

To make sure that these Yankee skippers kept their agreement and to see that no turbulent local patriots interfered with the operation, Admiral Graves detailed the cutter *Margaretta,* a schooner with a crew of forty and armed with four four-pounder cannon, to escort the two lumber schooners.

The ships reached Machias on June 2, 1775. Lieutenant Moore of the Royal Navy, commanding the *Margaretta,* made his presence felt immediately. First, he announced that anyone who was to have any of the supplies carried by the two schooners must sign a paper agreeing not to interfere with the procurement and loading of the lumber for Boston.

Moore was under the impression that the Machias people had not heard of the Lexington-Concord battle, but rumors and reports had reached them. The town was seething. A liberty pole was erected on the village green, whereupon Moore demanded that they cut it down or he would fire on the town. Although the people of Machias did not cut down the liberty pole, Moore did not wish to fire on the town until he had secured the two cargoes of lumber.

This the people of Machias did not intend to permit. Under the leadership of Benjamin Foster they held a meeting at the side of a brook east of the town to form plans. After a great many views had been aired, Foster said that he was going to jump over to the other side of the brook and every man who was ready to follow him in an attack on the two lumber schooners and the *Margaretta* would jump over after him.

The sixty men present leaped over the brook after him, and the place is to this day known as "Foster's Rubicon." The most economical plan seemed to them to capture Lieutenant Moore when he attended Sunday church service, and with him as a hostage, all would be easy.

Plans were made to surround the church and that they did. The scheme failed when a Negro servant saw from the church window some armed men crossing the river on logs. Suspecting he was soon to be in the midst of a fight, he let out a cry of alarm. One glance from the church window was enough for Moore. Knocking over several of the congregation in his haste, he leaped through the window and made for the water front at a run, well ahead of the pursuing citizens of Machias.

Immediately he was aboard, Moore gave orders to weigh anchor, and the *Margaretta* dropped downstream to the bay. The Americans did not have the slightest intention of letting the matter stop at this point. Seizing the two lumber schooners, they prepared to go after the British man-of-war. In one of them, the *Unity*, the crew numbered forty and the armament twenty guns, some of them fowling pieces. Those who did not have guns had axes, pitchforks, or scythe blades.

The *Unity* started down-river, followed by the *Falmouth Packet* under the command of Captain Benjamin Foster. They had not progressed far when Foster's vessel ran hard aground. Unfortunate this was, yet it did not discourage the forty men aboard the *Unity*. They kept on.

At about this time, with their leader, Benjamin Foster, in a vessel now motionless with its keel stuck fast in a mudbank, the *Unity*'s crew suddenly realized they had no captain. Fast approaching the enemy ship *Margaretta*, they held one of the speediest elections on record. As a result, the new captain was Jeremiah O'Brien, the oldest son of Morris. His election will appear the less surprising when we realize that the vessel's crew contained not only all six O'Brien boys, but also the three young men who had married the three O'Brien girls. Morris, the father of the clan, who had very much wanted to be in the fight, they had with difficulty persuaded to stay ashore.

That this choice of a captain was not mere politics was soon apparent. Captain Jeremiah, realizing they were shortly to be under fire, ordered his men to build a long bulwark or shield of pine boards as a protection against enemy musketry and grapeshot. Then he made for the *Margaretta*.

What followed was a sharp naval action. The *Unity's* bowsprit pierced the mainsail of the Britisher, and John O'Brien, eager to be first on the enemy's deck, leaped and made it. Then the ships separated, leaving John alone with the English firing muskets at him and charging him with bayonets. John wasted not a second. Diving overboard an instant before being skewered by a British bayonet, he swam to the *Unity,* seized a line thrown to him and scrambled back aboard, still with a whole hide.

Captain Jeremiah O'Brien ordered his helmsman to steer to come alongside the enemy and then he directed his men to use what little ammunition they had on the man at the *Margaretta's* wheel and on Lieutenant Moore, the commanding officer. Moore had the same idea. Using hand grenades, in that day nearly as deadly as they are now, he went after O'Brien. The two grenades he threw did not explode near enough to the captain to injure him; then, before the lieutenant could throw another, a ball from a Yankee musket felled him.

At the same moment the British helmsman was hit and

sank limply over his wheel. Moore was a brave man in the best tradition of Britain's superb Royal Navy, but his second in command, Midshipman Stillingfleet, was not worthy to command even a dory. Terrified, he fled below.

The *Unity* now came alongside the enemy, grappled and made fast. The Machias men, including the nine of the O'Brien family, swarmed over the side with their guns and axes and pitchforks. Now leaderless and with half a dozen of their number lying bleeding on the deck, the British crew surrendered and threw down their weapons.

Thus ended the first naval engagement of the American Revolution, a complete victory for this crew of colonists, a quarter of which consisted of the O'Briens and their in-laws. The captured *Margaretta* was brought into Machias, and her wounded were carried ashore there to be given the best care this frontier town could furnish. The valiant Lieutenant Moore expired in spite of what they could do for him. The Machias people even dispatched a vessel to Nova Scotia in an attempt to procure a good surgeon, but by the time he arrived, Moore was dead.

He was a worthy foe, and everyone on the American side regretted that his death was one of the results of their victory. He was to have been married soon to a girl in Halifax, which brought home to everyone, as much as the loss of some of their own townsmen, the tragedy that comes with war.

This battle was called the "Lexington of the Sea" because it was the first naval clash between the Royal Navy and an American ship. Naturally the news of it, as it slowly spread from this remote frontier place to the thirteen colonies, was the occasion of much rejoicing.

It was a proud victory for Captain Jeremiah O'Brien and

his men, for Machias, for the whole American cause. Yet it
is difficult to understand how a British man-of-war with four
cannon, plenty of small arms and a disciplined crew could
have been taken by a schooner manned by rustics carrying
few muskets, short of gunpowder, and with only pitchforks
and axes for close work.

On the credit side for the Americans is the shield of pine
boards protecting the men from musket fire, the fighting
spirit of Jeremiah O'Brien, his skill in handling his vessel,
his generalship in ordering his crew to concentrate what little ammunition they had on Lieutenant Moore, the commander, and on the British helmsman. Added to this was
the fierce spirit of these forty American frontiersmen, un-
disciplined in war, yet charged with the conviction that here
they were striking at the British government which was op-
pressing them.

And on the debit side for the British was a failure to understand that an American fighting force could be dangerous. Why every English officer thought Americans not only
lacked skill in all military matters but were a cowardly lot,
incapable of facing an enemy in battle, is not clear to us at
this time. Possibly colonial troops acted poorly in some of
the battles in the French and Indian War, although we have
no record of such occasions. Maybe this notion stemmed from
the condescending arrogance which, in the midst of a host
of good qualities, is to be found in the English character.
This attitude toward armed Americans was apparent in the
British on the day of Concord and Lexington, again at Bunker Hill. Only after a series of dreadfully expensive lessons
did Englishmen relinquish the idea that any unit of American fighting men, ashore or afloat, was a "rabble in arms."

The unfortunate Moore should have used his four-pounder cannon on Jeremiah O'Brien's approaching *Unity*. Easily he could have disabled the American ship. But he did not take them seriously. He thought a little gunfire and some grenades would make them sheer off and flee.

Then when Moore fell, the command passed to the wretched Stillingfleet, and he fled below decks. Such cowardly officers were practically unknown in the Royal Navy. What became of Stillingfleet is not recorded. A midshipman, he was doubtless very young and therefore probably cashiered in disgrace instead of being court-martialed and shot. The crew, without a leader, utterly unused to the idea that Americans could swarm aboard with such impetuous courage, appeared to have collapsed and were led away into captivity.

For Jeremiah O'Brien there were to be more chapters of American naval history, enough so that the United States Navy, when it adopted the practice of naming destroyers for naval heroes, christened one of them the *O'Brien*. The British, enraged when they learned of the loss of the *Margaretta*, sent two warships from Halifax to deal with O'Brien and the rest of the rebellious Machias people. HMS *Diligence*, eight guns, and HMS *Tapanagouche*, sixteen swivels, were crossing the Bay of Fundy on this mission when they met up with Captain O'Brien's *Unity*.

He had mounted the *Margaretta*'s four-pounders on his ship and he had with him Benjamin Foster's *Falmouth Packet*, which had run aground on her way to the first battle. Here again O'Brien's superb leadership was apparent, for he so maneuvered that he was able to attack each British ship separately. Again victorious, he captured both and brought them in on July 12, 1775.

For this brilliant victory the Massachusetts Provincial Assembly, sitting at Watertown, made Jeremiah O'Brien a captain in the State Marine. He continued to fight the British at sea, recapturing American ships which had been taken by the Royal Navy, and on one occasion gathering in two enemy barges with thirty-five sailors and an officer. So annoyed was Admiral Graves that he sent out a squadron of four men-of-war under the command of the infamous Captain Mowatt to "overawe," as he put it, the pestiferous rebels along the coast of Maine. Villages were burned, including Falmouth (now Portland), and great hardships were inflicted on a populace on the verge of a severe northern winter. These exploits, however, completely lacked any military value.

Meanwhile Jeremiah O'Brien continued to sail the seas in privateers until 1780, when luck at last ran out. His privateer *Hannibal* was captured by two British frigates, and he was imprisoned in the ill-famed prison hulk *Jersey* at New York.

From this foul jail he was transported to England and immured in Mill Prison, where he was singled out for specially harsh punishment, although the barbarous treatment of any man unfortunate enough to be a prisoner of England was bad enough.

In Mill Prison Jeremiah O'Brien seemed to deteriorate. He was unshaven, dirty; his clothes were rags, and the victor of the "Lexington of the Sea" became more an animal than a man. The guards kicked him around contemptuously and paid little attention to this fellow who now slunk around corners of the prison yard.

One day they missed this wreck of a man at lockup time. They could not seem to recall having seen him in the yard during the afternoon. Then one of them did remember one fellow they had not seen before, clean shaven, nattily dressed, and they recalled wondering who he was and what he was doing there. An officer of the prison was called.

At last they pieced together what had happened, when they found Jeremiah's old clothes in his cell. Freshly shaved, dressed in the good clothes he had saved, he had appeared as a stranger, and when the gate had opened for some purpose, he had sauntered away.

Nor did they ever see him again, which is fortunate for Captain O'Brien, for a windowless dungeon would surely have been his lot. Once again he was too much for the British. He made his way across the Channel, and then he got passage to America, after a long wait.

Jeremiah O'Brien did not again sail against the British. By the time he had reached this country and had gone to Machias to tell his fiery old father where he had been all this time, the battle of Yorktown had been fought and the war was over.

History's pages were closed for him and his clan, at least the spectacular pages. Life was quiet now for the O'Briens, but Machias in the state of Maine has not forgotten them, and their descendants still live here. There is a Fort O'Brien, and O'Brien Brook, a pamphlet about them and the O'Brien Graveyard, where forty of them of that day and since sleep in the shade of the tall trees beyond any sound of saws cutting great logs into lumber or musketry and cannon fire driving the enemy away from this rugged land.

2

The Battle That Was Not Fought

IN EARLY 1775 the tension between the British government and the colonists who thought they were as good as any other Englishmen continued to increase. It had reached the point where the Massachusetts people had a military unit in every town, called the Minutemen, and they were collecting gunpowder, musket balls, and cannon which had been captured in the French and Indian War.

This was a situation which no government could permit to continue. General Gage, who commanded a sizable British army in Boston, tried to meet this ever-growing menace by sending troops, often in regimental strength, on sweeps through the countryside, searching out military supplies.

The Redcoats found little, for the Americans had an excellent, although unorganized, intelligence service. The word was "the regulars are out," carried well ahead of the British as their smart formations marched over the colonial roads to the beat of their drummers and the squeal of their fifers. Long before the lines of colorful uniforms and glittering bayonets arrived at the spot where spies said there was a depot of gunpowder or cannon or provisions, the Americans had

14

whisked their stores away to a new place of hiding.

The British army from these sweeps got plenty of healthful exercise and training, much needed after being pent up in the Boston garrison. The colonials got training, too, in the military art of being an "army of observation." Each time everyone wondered whether one army would run into the other under circumstances that would result in an exchange of hot lead and the shedding of blood.

So things stood on that last Sunday of February in 1775. This time it was Salem that was to be searched. Here in the largest seaport on the Yankee coast, except Boston, the patriots had been unusually industrious in accumulating military supplies. It was a prosperous town, so they had the means, and it was a very seditious one.

This time General Gage decided the American colonists were not to be given advance warning by scouts who galloped ahead of his marching column. The Redcoats were to go aboard ships of the Royal Navy, which would sail under sealed orders. Then the colonists would suddenly discover the Redcoats pouring ashore, too late to hurry about and conceal their illegal stores of ammunition and artillery.

Colonel Leslie's 64th Regiment was given the assignment of gathering in the supplies at Salem. Silently the soldiers boarded ship and departed from Boston, their destination unadvertised. One flaw lay in this plan. Salem harbor is at the most western part of a bay in which islands, ledges, sand bars and shoals are so plentiful that only a mariner who knows those waters thoroughly can get a ship safely alongside Derby Wharf. And British men-of-war were larger than Salem's merchantmen, which, although they might call at Canton and Batavia and Naples and Cape Town, were usually of less than three hundred tons burden.

No British captain cared to try to take a ship into Salem Bay where it might run aground, list so the big guns would not bear and then be the target of riflemen on the shore or possibly artillery. Every English officer was aware of the temper of the people. They knew there was coming a time when guns would speak; no naval officer wished to be aboard a vessel hard aground near shore when that time arrived.

So Colonel Leslie's 64th Regiment did not sail into Salem Bay. Instead the ships hove to off Marblehead Neck, which faces the open sea, lowered their boats and proceeded to put the troops ashore. The weather was excellent, and the ships stood well offshore. All danger of running aground or striking a ledge in the narrow and difficult waters of Salem Bay was thus avoided.

The Redcoats were landed during church time on this late-February morning. The colonials were religious people, faithful in their attendance at church. Possibly the British high command had it in mind that the landing of the troops would achieve greater surprise because everyone would be at morning services and therefore the landing might for a while go unobserved.

Any King's officer who entertained such a notion was quite unaware of certain characteristics of the Marbleheaders. To say that they permitted themselves individual opinions in the matter of religious observances is to put it conservatively. Numerous townspeople, who should have been sitting in the pews listening to the parson tell what it is like to be ashore in hell, were in fact around and about, attending to chores they thought needed doing.

Some paused to watch the clockwork precision of the British landing operation and the smart way the platoons and companies assembled on the shore. The long, perfect lines of red uniforms and shining bayonets were indeed something to be admired, especially by these men of Colonel Glover's regiment, where uniforms were the clothing that each soldier happened to have available.

These men of Marblehead did not stand for long gawking at this brilliant spectacle of a red-coated British regiment assembling. Mariners all, they were trained to act quickly in an emergency. Hurrying away from rocky Marblehead Neck, they ran into town, passing the word. Then the drums began to roll, the drums of Glover's regiment, drums that were beaten by men who could make the instrument pound out a rhythm that keeps men marching long after they are ready to drop or who were able to sound the call of urgency that brings a man up out of a chair and running.

As the sound of the drums vibrated in the streets of the town, the people came pouring out of the churches into the bright February sunshine, nor was the parson the last man out. They did not know the purpose of this British landing. Perhaps the King had decided the time had come to burn the place, which would have surprised the Marbleheaders not at all, for the town seethed with rebellious sentiment and had raised an entire regiment of Minutemen.

Every man in the regiment soon had his musket, bullet pouch and powder horn. They were deployed behind barns and houses, in the bushes, under fish flakes and overturned dories, ready to give the King's troops a taste of Indian fighting the minute they set fire to the first house. The English, these men knew, hated Indian fighting.

Colonel Leslie's 64th Regiment did not stop in Marblehead; they marched through the west end of town with their drums thumping and fifes carrying a marching tune. Every man was in step, eyes front, muskets at the slant, uniforms all the same, no soldier wearing some different garment he happened to like, as did colonial troops whenever they felt like it. The men of Glover's regiment, in their places of concealment, watched this splendid outfit march by. They listened to the drums and almost felt like getting out there behind the British and keeping step.

Plainly this expedition marched not against Marblehead but against Salem. Over there were the cannon and the stores of gunpowder. Salem was the target of this powerful military force. As the drums grew fainter in the distance, one thought was in the mind of every man—how to get word to Salem, so the military supplies collected so carefully with months of effort might be hurried to a place of safety.

It was Major Pedrick, on horseback, who carried the word. His swift ride, although immortalized by no poet, was as thrilling as Paul Revere's and as important. He reached Salem far ahead of the marching British column, his horse all of a lather, and shouted out his message to everyone he saw. The word was carried quickly to those in command; orders were swiftly given and as quickly carried out. Anywhere he looked in Salem, Major Pedrick saw men on the dead run, on their way to see to the safety of the military stores. In the distance he heard the beat of drums, summoning the Salem Minutemen to duty. Clearly his message had reached the proper authorities; he relaxed and led his exhausted horse to a stable.

The Salem people wasted no time. Their cannon and shot and powder barrels were trundled out of the warehouses, loaded onto drays and carried across the North River up back of town and on into Danvers to a place of hiding in a deep oak forest. Then they raised the drawbridge over the North River and waited.

It was not long before Colonel Leslie and his troops entered Salem—a handsome sight, the red against the white of the snow, the heads all bobbing along as if they were set on one frame, shoulders moving together, legs, arms, everything in rhythm. The Americans watched; they heard the measured scuff and crunch of army boots in the snow and gravel, the creak of the leather belts and cartridge boxes, the orders of the sergeants, and wondered who ever taught men to march that well.

When Leslie's column reached Salem Courthouse, they halted while the colonel and his staff talked to some Salem men. Here an exceedingly acrid argument took place. Hammond, a corpulent man in a flowered waistcoat, was one of the most active Tories. John Felt, a noted patriot, could and did shout as loudly as Hammond. Hammond informed Colonel Leslie that the cannon, powder and ball had been hurried across the North River but minutes before his arrival.

John Felt, a man who feared no one, faced Leslie, giving him a lecture on the rights of free men, particularly those of Salem. He went on to say that the 64th Regiment had no business to be here and then took the time to call Hammond a variety of names. That John Felt was not put under arrest then and there was due solely to the fact that feelings had not yet sharpened quite enough for that. General Gage, in Boston, was trying to do his duty by the King and do it gently enough to avoid war. Not yet was it time to cast a seditious scoundrel such as Felt into a dungeon.

Colonel Leslie soon tired of words. At an order his men came to attention, shouldered arms and marched off toward the North Bridge a quarter mile away, their drums thumping out a smart step. The drawbridge was up, and the Salem infantry were on the far side of the narrow river, not smart and in formation, like the Redcoats, but a long, straggling line, thin in some places, bunched up in others. Their appearance was not very military, but they looked mean, with their long guns and oddly assorted work clothes.

The drawbridge was up at enough of an angle so a ship from Blubber Hollow, upstream, might have passed through. At the top of the draw, his head visible, his body concealed by the thick planking, was David Mason, posted there by Colonel Pickering of the Salem regiment.

"Lower the bridge in the name of the King," bellowed Leslie.

"No, by ginger," roared Mason.

"You are obstructing a King's highway," boomed Leslie. "Lower that bridge."

"We built this highway and we didn't see the King around while we was working," retorted Mason, whose remarks were freer because he was protected from British bullets by the thick oak planks of the draw.

"I have orders to cross that bridge," the colonel announced, "and I'm going to stay here until I do cross it."

"Stay as long as you like," shouted Mason. "Stay until hell freezes over."

Most of the people of Salem were crowded down by the river by this time, standing behind the British troops. Whenever Leslie spoke, they let out a chorus of boos and catcalls and other impolite noises. Whatever Mason said they cheered.

At this time some of the Salem people jumped into three flat-bottomed boats hauled up on the British side of the river and began smashing the bottoms with axes so the Redcoats could not use them to cross.

Leslie's temper now became short. He snapped out an order; some of his troops with leveled muskets charged down to where the men were smashing the boats, bayonets fixed, and the Salem men ran, several with bleeding posteriors. In later years some historian asserted this to be the first bloodshed of the Revolution. Little attention was ever given this claim, perhaps because the wounds were serious enough only to require that the victims eat their meals from a mantelpiece for a few days, or possibly because wounds in that part of the anatomy did not seem of a dignity entitling these men to a place in the pages of our national history.

The affair now reached a critical point. Colonel Leslie was defied by the men on the other side of the river. He was being hooted and jeered by a mob on his own side of the river. John Felt was at his elbow, still giving voice with the arguments of the American cause. Parson Barnard stood near him, talking religion and peace and the rights of man.

It would not have been unnatural if Colonel Leslie had given the order to sweep Pickering's troops on the opposite shore with volleys of lead and chase the crowd on the Salem side with bayonets. He could have run John Felt through with his sword and he could have put the good Parson Barnard in irons. All this would have been not difficult with a regiment of trained British troops. A short, quick action would have swept Pickering's Salem regiment out of the way; then Leslie would be on the other side of the river, ready to march forward. But he did not know where these military supplies had gone. He might search all the way to Haverhill and not find them. And there was a more urgent consideration.

The road on the opposite side came down a gentle half-mile slope. From where he stood, Leslie had a long view and he saw the men coming with their muskets, not a marching column with drums and fixed bayonets and smart uniforms, but one man or two or three or a half dozen, approaching that river and turning off to the left or to the right to join the Salem infantry.

These were the Minutemen summoned by gun signals, bell signals, galloping riders fanning out north, west and south from Salem; the Minutemen prepared to set forth at a minute's notice to face the King's troops anywhere. From all over Essex County these men were coming. Leslie knew the country was rising. He faced a thousand men now; in another hour it would be two thousand. If he stayed the night in Salem, it might be ten thousand by sunrise. The alarm had gone as far as southern New Hampshire.

As for his line of retreat, it lay through hostile Salem, then through three miles of open country and woodland with the Minutemen of Beverly and Lynn on his flanks. Before he could reach his ships, he must fight his way through the Marblehead regiment.

As Colonel Leslie reviewed these considerations, these endless reinforcements straggled down the long slope and took their places facing him. He looked around him at the crowd of Salem people, unarmed, but pressing close. He cocked an eye at the afternoon sun low in the western sky. He had made his decision.

With Parson Barnard at his side, he shouted at David

Mason, perched on the raised drawbridge:

"If you lower the bridge, I'll agree to march my men fifty yards and then about-face."

Mason hesitated.

"Do it, Dave," shouted the parson. "The colonel has his orders to carry out. Let's settle this peacefully."

Mason said nothing.

"You can trust the colonel's word," boomed the parson in his best pulpit voice.

"We know it," allowed David Mason. "We'd trust Colonel Leslie quicker than his dratted King."

Colonel Pickering and his officers on the other side of the North River were talking it over, and every man held his breath while they consulted. The hooting, the howling of insults, the chatter ceased; there was dead silence, for everyone knew the decision for peace or war hung in the balance that very minute. Every American knew this English officer had to return to Boston with his orders carried out or he would not be an officer by this time on the morrow.

Further, every person present knew there were no braver troops than the British. Given the order, Leslie's men would plunge right into the North River, get across somehow and then fight to the last man. The decision now rested with Colonel Pickering. If he said "No," lead would begin to fly, the battle of Salem would commence, ending no one knew how, perhaps with this great town lying in ashes. Spectators were drifting away from points near the British 64th Regiment, seeking shelter behind trees and houses. Everywhere was tension, worried looks, people quietly withdrawing.

Then Pickering shouted an order; the windlasses were manned. Creaking, the bridge slowly came down with Mason still clinging to the edge. Orders rang out; the British shouldered arms. With drums beating and fifes squealing, colors flying, lines straight and never a man out of step, they set forth across the bridge. A splendid sight, these ordered ranks, bright uniforms and glittering bayonets, as their perfect formations tramped up the slope on the other side.

Yet a worrisome sight. Were they going to stop fifty yards beyond the bridge, as Leslie had agreed? Was his word good? Or was the battle to start on the other side of the North Bridge, instead of on the Salem side? And might some hot-headed patriot finger his trigger too hard and fire? The Minutemen watched—Salem men, Topsfield and Danvers and Wenham and Boxford men and those recently arrived from places as far away as Andover and Haverhill and Newbury.

No shot was fired. The 64th Regiment wheeled a short distance up the slope, and many a green young soldier in the ranks of the Minutemen was obliged to admire the beautiful way these troops executed the maneuver. They turned around and back down the slope they came. The planks of the North Bridge boomed to the tramp of their heavy boots, the drummers thumping out a marching rhythm that made the regiment step along as one man.

Then the fifes started another tune, a British favorite: "The World Turned Upside Down." Through Salem town they marched to that music, and when they reached North Street, Captain Eppes' Danvers Infantry was lined up at the side of the road. Somehow this entire unit had managed to get into Salem and take this position in the British rear.

When the Redcoats had passed, Captain Eppes barked an order and off went the Danvers Infantry, marching behind the British and to their music, a part of their column and stepping just as smartly. And the tune the British fifers played was appropriate, "The World Turned Upside Down," which it certainly was with British regulars retreating in the face of the colonial Minutemen. The British army had won victory on many European battlefields, yet here they turned away from a fight with these armed farmers and tradesmen and mariners. The Americans themselves were astounded.

The Danvers Infantry escorted Leslie out of Salem and then turned off. However, he was to be further honored. It was sunset when the 64th Regiment reached Marblehead. There at the roadside stood the entire Marblehead regiment, under arms, completely silent, eyes front. Not a Britisher turned his head as they swung by.

It is impossible, however, that Colonel Leslie could have failed to appraise this regiment of rough and ready mariners, each with his musket, a unit in much better military formation than any other group of Minutemen he had seen. Glad he was that he did not have to fight through these men to get back to his ships.

The last rank of British marched by; the regiment tramped out along the road to Marblehead Neck in the gathering dusk, and they were gone from the Yankee scene, with no further problem than to get into the boats and board their ships. This was February 28, 1775, the day the Revolution could have started in a furious battle on the north side of Salem. The battle could have commenced if Colonel Leslie had been more stubborn or hotheaded or if he had not kept his word and turned around after crossing the bridge.

It could have started if Colonel Pickering had been pigheaded or if Parson Barnard had not been there to preach peace to the British or if Colonel Leslie, in a moment of impatience, had ordered the Reverend Barnard to be led away.

Suppose Leslie had been in command at Lexington Green seven weeks later and suppose Colonel Pickering and Parson Barnard had been there. Or at the Concord Bridge. Would there have been a battle? The question is useless. In the New England countryside in 1775 two hostile armies were marching back and forth, one composed of men with a deep grievance, the other with orders to suppress rebellion.

They confronted each other at Salem; no shot was fired. Excellent officers worked out a compromise, and the sun went down on a scene of peace. This was no more than luck. The grievances remained; the armies continued to march. Again they confronted each other, and the deep, seething tensions burst forth like a dreadful volcano when a couple of Americans at Lexington squeezed their triggers. And if they had not fired and if Pitcairn's men had not returned the fire, the "shot heard round the world" would not have been fired on the nineteenth of April. But it would have been fired later, as the British marched on more of their sweeps through the countryside and as the American Minutemen became better organized and better armed and as the English Parliament and Ministry continued their unjust treatment of the American colonies, thus building resentment upon resentment.

3

The Concord Fight

THAT NIGHT of April 18, 1775, Paul Revere was staying up very late indeed, standing on the shore opposite from Boston with his eye on the steeple of the Old North Church. Word had it the British regulars were to march out to Concord to look for military stores accumulated by the Massachusetts militia, the Minutemen, against the day when they might have to fight the King's troops for their rights. In Boston a friend, one of the patriots, was to put one lantern in the belfry if the Redcoats were to move by land over Roxbury Neck and two lanterns if they crossed the harbor to Cambridge and marched in that direction.

"One if by land and two if by sea," Paul Revere had agreed with the man in Boston. "And I on the opposite shore will be." His mission was to notify all the towns between Cambridge and Concord that "the regulars are out," as the Americans phrased it when the British army staged one of its expeditions into the countryside to search for cannon, gunpowder, bullets and military provisions. "To ride and give the alarm to every Middlesex village and farm" was the task assigned to Revere.

27

Paul Revere did not wait there on the shore to no purpose. At last in the far belfry of the Old North Church he saw the two pin points of light, the signal hoisted by the devoted patriot who by careful intelligence had learned the British plan and thus had flashed word of it—a spy, in military parlance, who might have danced on air had he been caught while performing this vital service for the American cause. Revere hesitated not a moment. Swinging into the saddle, he was away, rapping on doors in the dead of night. As a sleepy head appeared at a bedroom window, he shouted his message, spurred onward his horse, and galloped along the highway, ever deeper into Middlesex County, giving the word. And as he rode, he heard behind him the results of his message: the ringing of bells in the church steeples, the firing of minute guns. The Minutemen had the news; the country was rising.

At Medford, on the upper reaches of the Mystic River, the organization of the Minutemen had swung into action by the time Revere was beyond the confines of the town, as long before planned. The bells rang, the minute guns were fired and horsemen saddled their mounts to ride into the country-side with the word that the British regulars were out. One rider headed for Malden. He pounded on the doors of the key men, then on he galloped toward Black Anne's Corner in the northernmost section of Chelsea.

Reaching the Boston Post Road, he turned into the Saugus part of Lynn, thumping on doors, shouting the news, then over the river, up Tower Hill, and into the center of Lynn. Beyond, in the easterly part of the town, later called Swamp-scott, he urged his lathered horse forward, still arousing householders, telling them to spread the news. Then on to

Marblehead and Salem he rode, while behind him church bells rang and minute guns fired in the night.

The Lynners turned out. In the Saugus end of town, the most westerly, Captain Parker's company gathered and were first on the march, because they were first to get the word. In the Lynnfield end of town, miles to the north, Captain Bancroft's men came from widely separated farms to their assembly point. In the center of Lynn the drummers and the fife of Captain Ezra Newhall's company made for the Common and played the long roll. In those days the drum was used for signals, and a good drummer was a necessity for relaying orders. The long roll was the order for assembly. Everyone in town knew what it meant. Men with their muskets, powder horns and bullet pouches came running from all directions as the drummers thumped out the message in the gray light of dawn.

By eight o'clock Newhall's company was on its way along the Post Road. Now the drummers beat a marching rhythm that made everyone forget he had jumped out of bed at an unearthly hour; feet scuffed along in the gravel—in step. Now and then another man came down a lane to join the company or ran from the rear to catch up.

Captain Mansfield's company was on the move, too, and in the eastern section, down Swampscott way, Captain Farrington's men were assembling. From the town of Lynn, wide in area but not populous, five companies of Minutemen were in motion toward Lexington and Concord.

In Captain Farrington's company were the three Ramsdell brothers, Shadrach, Meshach and Abednego. Marching along with the rest of the company were Shadrach and Meshach, but Abednego was not there. He and his friend Joe Richards, also of this company, had made plans to go duck shooting on this nineteenth day of April. They had risen long before dawn, taken their fowling pieces, and when sunrise came they were on the rocks of the bold and rugged Swampscott shore, far from any human habitation, scanning the sky for the first flight of ducks. Of the uproar in the town of Lynn they heard nothing.

Abednego Ramsdell and his friend Joe Richards came strolling down the road long after sunup, very much pleased with themselves, for luck had been good and each had three black ducks, enough for some very good eating. They were nearing home when they met Joe Richards' father, and then they heard the news of the rider who had galloped into Swampscott in the dawn with word that the British were marching on Lexington and Concord and all five Lynn companies were on the march.

Some idea of the morale of the Minutemen may be gained from the subsequent actions of these two men. Leaving the ducks with Mr. Richards, they set out at once to catch up with Captain Farrington's company. Ramsdell was later described by someone in the center of Lynn as running through town with his stockings fallen down to his shoe tops. Such was his eagerness to join his company that he did not stop to try to pull them up again. Ramsdell swung around by his house to get his musket, but Richards did not bother even to do that; he set out with the fowling piece he had used for shooting ducks.

From Swampscott to the road from Boston to Lexington and Concord is a long march, more than twelve miles, and these men had started late. Their company and the others from Lynn were well ahead of them. On the way they met other Minutemen, some from Lynn, some from other towns, who had not received the word in time to march with their companies. All were eager to catch up and be with their outfits when the time came to face the British. So they joined together, named one of their number as commander, and marched over Tower Hill through Saugus, past the towering rocky hill at Black Anne's Corner and into Malden and then Medford as a unit.

While the men from Lynn and Salem and Danvers and all the other towns distant from Lexington and Concord were marching over the road, indeed, even while the long roll of the drums was sounding on Lynn Common, things had been happening. In those same moments of dawn the Lexington men were in formation on the village green. Seven hundred British regulars, in all the glory of their brightly colored uniforms, came marching into Lexington, drums banging, fifes squealing, bayonets gleaming in the early light. These troops had been on the move all night, yet they moved in superb order, not a man out of step.

Then came the collision between Major Pitcairn's determined troops, who had been ordered not to fire, and the Minutemen, who likewise had been ordered not to fire. Never has it been settled who fired first. Certain only it is that here, for the first time in these months and years of strained, hair-trigger relations between the British English and the American English, the restraint gave way. Hot lead flew on Lexington Green. Americans lay dead on the grass; bleeding Minutemen dragged themselves away; British soldiers were wounded. This was war. In these moments the peace was shattered beyond repair.

The gunfire at Lexington ended, and the British marched

on to Concord to see to the main business of their expedition. There they built a fire of artillery wheels, tossed casks of bullets and barrels of flour into a pond, and sent out details to various spots to search for the large quantities of military supplies they had thought were here but somehow seemed not to be. At the North Bridge three companies of Redcoats stood guard while other companies went forward to search farms. As yet no shot had been fired at Concord, but a column of smoke began to rise from the town, rolling and tumbling the way it does when a very hot fire is burning.

Watching the British troops at the North Bridge were several companies of Minutemen. Nothing had happened; indeed, it seemed as if nothing would. It was the column of thick, dark smoke that changed the situation. The Minutemen assumed that the British had commenced to burn Concord and they did not intend to stand by and permit it. The order came to advance. To the beat of their drummers, the Americans marched in a column of twos down the slope toward Captain Laurie and his men at the bridge. The captain stared in amazement at this column of men in brown hunting shirts and farm clothes, not a man dressed like a soldier, muskets on their shoulders, in perfect step and getting nearer every second.

This armed mob was actually advancing against the British regular army. Captain Laurie gave the order to fire. The volley crashed out; the powder smoke hung heavy, and musket balls whined through the American ranks. Down went the captain of the Acton company and the drummer and many others. At once the Americans broke ranks, looking for cover as they had been taught to do when lead was flying. Not until they were on their bellies behind bushes and rocks and trees did they fire and then slowly and carefully.

The Redcoats stood at the bridge, erect, facing the enemy and blazing away at men they could scarcely see. Their doctrine was to fire volleys in the general direction of the enemy, never taking such careful aim as did the Americans, for they relied heavily on bayonet charges. The marksmanship of the Minutemen soon made the British position intolerable; red-uniformed bodies lay sprawled on the planking of the bridge.

The English troops broke and ran toward Concord, leaving their wounded comrades behind them. The Minutemen re-formed their column and marched toward the town, following the fleeing British troops. Possibly some of the local farmers and artisans in that American column of twos realized what that short march over the North Bridge and along the road beyond meant. The trained and disciplined and uniformed soldiers of the King, units victorious on many a European battlefield, were retreating before an outfit no one had ever heard of before, men called from their beds to get out here to defend the lands that were theirs, farmers and shoemakers and blacksmiths who fought like Indians. It did not seem real even to those who comprehended what had happened.

Then the Minutemen, following the Redcoats at a distance, discovered that the smoke came from burning artillery wheels in the middle of the street. The British had not commenced to burn Concord. For a considerable time at Concord it seemed as if the firing at the North Bridge might turn out to be no more than an episode, a flare-up like the Boston Massacre.

The Americans drew off to a nearby hill. Soon the four British companies sent off to search various farms for concealed arms and gunpowder came marching back toward town. The Americans on the hill let them pass; not a shot was fired. Soon afterward, when the entire force of British regulars began to march out of Concord, headed back to Boston, it looked like the end of any doings for this day.

The companies of Minutemen followed the English troops down the Lexington road, staying at a distance, making no hostile move. With every mile the number of American soldiers swarming over the countryside increased. The companies from Carlisle and Chelmsford and Reading and Littleton were on the scene; others were arriving every few minutes.

Still not a shot was fired. In spite of the fight on Lexington Green and the sharp, short battle at the North Bridge, it seemed as if the Americans were no more than seeing the British home. The last of the red-coated grenadiers were crossing a little bridge. They looked back. Everywhere they saw Minutemen—on the road, in the fields, in the woods, up on the ridge. The countryside was alive with armed men. It may be a British officer thought a volley would make these bumpkins keep their distance; perhaps he was just tired of looking at Minutemen whichever way he turned his head, or possibly he yearned for action. At an order the grenadiers fired a volley, turned and marched on.

Only this volley was needed to set every American in the area to firing. Until this moment they had seemed to feel that if there were no more firing, these two fights that had already occurred might somehow be overlooked. To fire on the King's troops seemed wrong, rebellious, even irreverent. Carefully they had refrained from taking even one shot at the retreating British soldiers. But they were yearning for action, and this volley seemed to change everything. Now from behind trees, bushes, stone walls and barns came puffs of powder smoke as the Americans sought cover and took aim.

When the Redcoats began to drop, their comrades helped them along. The flying lead got thicker, and the King's troops were taking hard punishment. Faster they moved, firing as they neared Lexington, but they could not spot the Americans, who had been taught concealment by generations of Indian fighting. Even where they could see one of the Minutemen their hits were few, for the British were better bayonet fighters than marksmen. They were running as they entered Lexington.

There the rest of the Boston garrison were waiting. Lieutenant Colonel Smith early in the morning had sent a message to General Gage in Boston that the country was up in arms and he asked for reinforcements. Every available British regular was sent out under the command of Lord Percy. He had two cannon and fired a few blasts of grapeshot at the Americans who speedily took to the woods.

Then Lord Percy with his one thousand fresh troops set out for Boston, sheltering the tired and bedraggled men who had been marching and fighting since midnight. No sooner had Percy limbered up his cannon and started to move than the Americans commenced firing again, as before from every place of concealment they could find. The British ordeal was dreadful, and everywhere in the ranks men were dropping. The road was bloody and soldiers in red uniforms lay here and there. The King's troops were in too much of a hurry now to pick them up. So the fight went down the road from Lexington to the little town of Menotomy, which today is called Arlington.

None of the facts of the battle were known to the Lynn

companies as they neared the end of their more than twelve miles of marching, nor had the Danvers companies, who marched near them, heard a word of news. These Minutemen knew only that the British had marched to Lexington and Concord and that the road ran through Menotomy.

At last the Lynn and Danvers men reached the highway from Boston. There they stopped to rest and consider their next step. Certain it was that the Redcoats had not returned, although it was afternoon. One course of action would have been to march toward Lexington and Concord and meet the British. The Americans knew better. A head-on collision with the enemy would have resulted in a bayonet fight, and the Minutemen had few bayonets. Even had they been equipped with bayonets, it would have been folly to have used them, for the English Army were probably the best bayonet fighters in the world. Their enemies on many a European battlefield had learned that to their sorrow.

It seemed wiser to fight the battle that was coming in the American way. Therefore the men spread out and sought cover in positions giving them a clear shot at the road when the Redcoats appeared. Some of the Danvers men found an excellent place behind a big pile of shingles here on the Jason Russell farm. They waited, the Lynn men and the Danvers men, muskets at the ready.

Abednego Ramsdell and Joseph Richards, who at last had caught up with their comrades in Captain Farrington's company, waited with the rest, wondering where the British were and what had happened up Concord way. Rumors of the fight on Lexington Green and the casualties were numerous here in Menotomy, so it was plain to everyone that this was to be no mere march, such as Colonel Leslie's expedition to Salem in late February.

At last, in the distance, they heard it: the sound of gunfire, steady, never ceasing, single shots, groups of shots, sometimes a volley. They fingered their triggers, waiting, as the minutes ticked by and the shots became louder, nearer. Then, far down the road, the first red uniforms appeared in the distance, more of them and still more, filling the road from one side to the other, more British soldiers than any man there had ever seen before.

The Lynners and the Danvers men smiled as they waited to select their targets in the fast approaching British ranks. Then, in one horrible moment, the Minutemen had a dreadful lesson in the cruel art of war. From their rear a volley crashed. Danvers men behind the pile of shingles fell; the glass in the windows of the rear of the Jason Russell house was shattered; Lynn men fell on all sides.

From the woods charged the British Light Infantry, bayonets fixed, yelling and screaming. They were the flankers, whose mission it was to protect the marching column by making wide sweeps through fields and bushes and woods on each side. The Light Infantry had been having a hard day of it, fighting Americans concealed behind trees and in thickets all the way from Concord, and they had suffered many casualties.

Now they had found a situation very much to their liking: an enemy so intent on something else that they had given no thought to their rear. Wildly the British used their bayonets after firing their volley. Seven of the Danvers company were killed and five of the Lynn men. Jason Russell himself, appearing in the doorway, was run through with a bayonet and left on his own steps with his life ebbing away.

The British Light Infantry moved out with great swiftness

before the Minutemen all around them could recover from their surprise and concentrate on them their deadly musketry fire. Abednego Ramsdell, who only this morning had been shooting black ducks along the rugged shores of Swampscott, lay dead in the farmyard.

His companion, Joe Richards, had fired one shot with his fowling piece. He had loaded it with a charge suitable, he thought, to bring down not a duck but a British grenadier. Richards had, however, overloaded his gun. It blew up in his hands, and he was lucky enough to escape with minor burns. With the remains of his weapon he clubbed a British Light Infantryman who was about to run his bayonet into the prostrate form of Abednego Ramsdell. The man fled, holding onto his forearm where Richards' gun barrel had struck him.

The mission of these British flankers was to hit fast and keep up with their main column on the road, so they did not continue the fight around the Jason Russell house. They moved out on the double, leaving behind them twelve dead Americans and as many wounded. Little had the Lynn and Danvers men done to trouble the main British column as it passed. They had been too busy preserving their own lives before this desperate bayonet charge.

The fight swirled on down the road toward Boston. Joe Richards helped the others move the dead into the house, where all twelve of them were laid out in a row in the front room and with them Mr. Russell, whose house this was. Then, with a hard light in his eyes, Richards, now with no weapon, went out into the road and trudged off toward Boston after the retreating British. In the distance he could hear the constant crackle of musket fire.

He had not gone far before he found a badly wounded

British grenadier lying at the roadside, the blood from a gaping leg wound turning the grass beneath him red. Richards stopped, and with the enemy's shirt and strips from his own and a stick from the roadside bushes, he fashioned a tourniquet as he had seen an old woodsman do it for a man with an ax wound. The bleeding gradually stopped as he turned the stick to tighten up the bandage.

"Boy, I think you're going to stay in America," observed Joe. "Keep your hand on the stick. Slack off on it once in a while and let a little blood run, then tighten up. Stay here until you're picked up, keep a civil tongue in your head, and you'll end up owning a piece of land a few score miles west of here. Then you'll be an American."

Richards then helped himself to the man's musket and bayonet, his bullets and his gunpowder, and set off on the double to catch up with the battle. He wanted to get within gunshot of the English Light Infantry and use this new musket of his on them. He figured he owed them one, more than one, for his friend Abednego who lay dead in the front room of the big farmhouse back there.

He followed the fight and caught up. He fired again and again and thought he got hits, yet there was no way of being sure, for there were now so many Minutemen with him, pecking away at the rear of the enemy column. Certain it was that as they fired many a Britisher went down. Several times before the fight reached Charlestown and the protection of the guns of the English men-of war, Joe Richards and those with him picked up one of the men they had shot down and worked over him with such first aid as they could devise. Then, leaving the casualty in a comfortable place or turning him over to a kind-hearted housewife, they took his weapons and ammunition and hurried on toward the sound of battle.

The day's fighting ended at salt water. The ships of the Royal Navy fired broadsides of grapeshot and round shot at the Americans, driving them out of range. The beaten British, with hundreds of wounded and many lying dead along the miles toward Lexington, were utterly exhausted. Neither the officers nor the men of these proud regiments with a long tradition of victory could understand how they had ever taken such a trouncing from an enemy that at no time during this whole long day had looked much like anything one could call an army.

Now the British army found themselves prisoners in Boston, for the Minutemen stayed, forming a ring around the town. Not all remained; some went home and others replaced them to keep enough of a military force so that the King's Army was confined. And this was the way the situation continued until that day in the following March when the British sailed away, never to return.

One day, June 17, the British tried to break the ring that imprisoned them. They took Bunker Hill in Charlestown, and Breed's Hill. The cost was ghastly and the ring around Boston did no more than bulge a little. It did not break. In this battle on April 19, a battle no one planned to start, a battle which, once started, seemed to be about to dwindle away, England's mighty empire lost a vast territory.

Before Paul Revere saw the two lanterns in the belfry of the Old North Church, all of New England had belonged to the King of England. By sundown of the nineteenth the entire area, except Boston, had ceased to be his. Never again did British troops set foot in New England except momentarily in coastal raids in Maine and on that famous day at Bennington, Vermont. It was a military disaster brought about by the swarms of colonial militia—a rabble in arms, as one contemptuous British officer described them.

The British casualties were very heavy. As for the Minutemen, the cost of this great victory varied greatly among the companies. The Lexington men suffered heavily in those few minutes at dawn on their village green. At the North Bridge the Acton company lost its captain and its drummer. Some companies had scarcely a casualty. One of the heaviest prices was paid by the men from Lynn and Danvers in Essex County.

They had marched all morning, completely ignorant of the affair on Lexington Green and the sharp battle at the North Bridge. Arriving at the Jason Russell house in Menotomy in the afternoon, they still knew only that some fighting had taken place. Taking a position, as was their duty, they were ready to join in the battle as they heard it growing nearer and nearer.

Had they been led by experienced officers, they would have been on their guard against the flanking movement of the British Light Infantry. It was a standard and well-known tactic. But their officers were not seasoned fighters, not then. Therefore the surprise was complete when these splendidly trained and disciplined troops suddenly appeared in their rear and swept down on them. The Minutemen fought valiantly and suffered heavily.

After the battle the Lynn companies and the Danvers companies returned home, bearing their dead in borrowed wagons. The Lynn men took Abednego Ramsdell and the others to their people. The Danvers men were laid out in one house in Danversport and their folks, notified, came down to get them. This was a black day for these families. It was to be years before they could come to realize that the boys who had been torn from them this day had fallen in one of the most significant victories ever won by the people of this continent.

4

Ring around Boston

TO UNDERSTAND the battle of Bunker Hill on June 17, 1775, requires a close look at the Concord and Lexington fight, about two months before. On that nineteenth day of April the country literally had "risen," to use the phrase appearing in British reports of the engagement.

This uprising struck the strong British force that marched out to Concord like a series of sledge-hammer blows. In one of the most astonishing battles in military history, an expedition composed of what were considered among the best troops in the world was heavily defeated by colonial militia with little training.

Yet the reasons are simple. First, the American colonists had a superb signal system that alerted every local company of militia and brought it to the scene in an unbelievably short time. This signal system is brilliantly described in Longfellow's poem *Paul Revere's Ride*. Second, these local militia, the Minutemen, although not trained to anywhere near the extent of regular troops, were strong, hardy characters accustomed to the use of guns and with an excellent morale founded on a very clear idea of why they were fighting.

And the third reason is the lesson these English colonials, living in a country where the wilderness was not far away, had learned in their fights with the Indians. The bitter war with the French and Indians was not long ended, and there the Americans discovered that to live they had to take advantage of every bit of cover. This lesson has remained a part of American military doctrine to this day, as the Germans found out in a painful way on the old Western Front and in the Second World War in the forests along their borders.

So the companies of Minutemen struck from scores of ambushes and chased the Redcoats back into Boston on that bloody nineteenth of April. Then it was that the Americans found they were confronted with a situation they had never contemplated. They had an army in the field, whereas all their plans were based on local companies of Minutemen ready for instant action. They had the entire British army penned up in Boston, besieged, which they had never intended to do. In fact, they had never intended to fight the King's troops at all. Events had taken charge.

And as a result of events the Americans had forged a ring of troops around Boston, militia companies facing the British army from Roxbury through Cambridge to Prospect Hill on the north. There were a general headquarters, supply depots and billets for the troops, picket lines confronting the British, and every road was blockaded.

This assemblage of local companies of Minutemen transformed into an army had besieged Boston for two months without being tested and the day of trial had to come. On that one day of Concord and Lexington the King had lost all of New England. Without breaking the ring around Boston these provinces were lost forever.

The Americans got word of the British plan to burst through the ring. The Redcoats were to move across Boston harbor, occupy Charlestown, then march on Cambridge, smash the center of the American army, capture its headquarters and supply depots and disperse this rebellious rabble. General Ward immediately ordered a regiment to occupy Charlestown, which is on a peninsula that is almost an island, lying across the narrowest part of the harbor from Boston and attached to the mainland by a narrow stem of land, like a pear hanging from a tree.

Colonel Prescott's regiment was sent to Charlestown to block the British. They marched to the Harvard College grounds, where President Langdon led them in prayer. Then off they went, with a few wagons loaded with picks and shovels. Joining them were details from Bridge's and Frye's regiments and a couple of hundred Connecticut men under Captain Knowlton. General Israel Putnam was in this column and so was Colonel Gridley, a military engineer who could lay out a fort as easily as most of these men could lay out a barn.

The long column of men marched off into the night, scuffing along the gravel and dust of the narrow Charlestown road, muskets slung over their shoulders and knapsacks bulging with rations. Their orders were to fortify Bunker Hill. They knew that when General Gage saw their fort in the morning there would be a big fight. They had no orders as to what to do then. They knew.

Not in the whole world was there an army that cared to face the British regulars on an open battlefield. The last who had tried it, the French at Minden, had been horribly defeated. Everyone knew about that battle. Yet the Americans meant to challenge the British.

In one short June night the knoll called Breed's Hill was fortified. Between sundown and sunup a fortress was built in complete darkness and with so little commotion that the watch on the British man-of-war anchored in the stream called out "All's well" on the hour and the half-hour. Then dawn came. The gray shades grew lighter; details appeared, and then full daylight showed everything as it was: this hill crowned by a strong fortification where at sunset it had been bare.

If the Americans who had labored through the night to build this redoubt had wondered what the British reaction would be when they saw it, their answer came with thunderous promptitude. From the English warships in the harbor, broadsides crashed forth, using every cannon that could be brought to bear. Then the floating batteries, barges mounting cannon, joined in the hellish uproar.

This was the first time the Americans had ever faced strong artillery fire, and there was a question whether they could hold their position under this massive cannonading. The commanding officers had worried about the reaction of their inexperienced troops, but at last they had their answer. None of these Minutemen broke and ran. Great showers of dirt flew as the balls struck the earthen walls, but the men crouched in safety. One man, who for a reason never ascertained had left the protection of the redoubt, was struck by a cannon ball and his remains, in two halves, lay upon the grass of the slope. There were no other casualties as six warships and floating batteries cannonaded.

When it was clear to the British that this tremendous barrage had done nothing whatsoever to dislodge the Americans, the whole of the King's army came across Boston harbor in boats. The marines from the H.M.S. *Somerset* joined them, and they lined up on the Charlestown shore, a most brilliant and varied collection of bright uniforms. To many a Minuteman crouched in the redoubt it seemed unreal that they were actually to fight these troops, the bravest, the best in the world.

It was very real to Colonel Prescott, however. He strode along the parapet, giving orders to his men.

"Hold your fire," he shouted as the long lines of British started forward, drums thumping, fifes playing, lines perfect, every musket aslant at the same angle, bayonets glittering in the sun.

"Don't fire until you get the order," commanded Colonel Prescott, up on the rampart and looking down at his men. "Get those handsomely dressed officers first. Any man who fires without orders will feel the point of this sword."

"That's right," yelled Israel Putnam. "Don't fire until you see the whites of their eyes."

The men behind the earthen walls watched the lines of Redcoats come nearer, step by step. They heard the order and saw the British muskets come off the shoulders in one motion. They fired, and a hail of leaden bullets spattered against the earthen walls of the redoubt, while some whined overhead. Americans never were able to understand a British volley, fired without aiming from positions where damage to the enemy was unlikely. A Yankee settler out hunting who used his gun that way would bring back nothing to feed his family. The Americans concluded that the Redcoats were such poor shots because in England only the rich were allowed to go hunting and so the ordinary man got no experience with a gun.

The men behind the walls of the redoubt on Breed's Hill, however, were not inclined to think about things theoretical at this particular time. The bayonets were coming nearer with every step these long red lines of men took; wicked bayonets with fourteen-inch blades, long enough to go into a man's belly and come out of his back. Every man there hated the thought of these British weapons. A couple could stand the suspense of these silently advancing Redcoats no longer. They fired and others were ready to fire, but Colonel Prescott was on the rampart, kicking up the leveled musket barrels.

"Wait for the order," he yelled. "Do you want I should run you through with my sword?"

There was no more firing from the redoubt on Breed's Hill. Now plainly visible were the faces of the advancing British: hard, grim faces behind that solid line of bayonets. In seconds they would be over the rampart. Then came the order.

"Fire."

The roar from the redoubt was like a cannon, and powder smoke spouted out ahead in a thick, foglike cloud. The men could see nothing as they hurried to reload, yet they knew what had happened from the shouts and shrieks and moans from the slopes in front of their fort. As the thick powder smoke drifted away, what they saw made many a man sick.

The line of red uniforms, beautiful even though they spelled death if ever they came over the ramparts, now lay broken, smashed into fragments by the storm of lead from the American muskets. Out there some bodies lay still while others writhed on the ground. Some men still standing wandered around as if lost.

Had the entire British line been made of scarlet crockery and then kicked over by some drunken fellow, the destruction could have been no worse. The Americans fired now as they reloaded, unevenly rather than in one crashing volley, yet a heavy fire knocked over men who still stood. The British retreated toward the beach on which they had landed, well out of range, where they could again line up in a military formation.

At the same time as this frontal attack, the British Light Infantry tried to flank the American left by marching along the shore of the Mystic River. There they ran into Stark's New Hampshire troops, who used the same tactics of holding their fire until the enemy was close upon them. On the right, from the houses of Charlestown, the Yankee sharpshooters fired from concealed positions.

Although this was a moment of victory, few were the Americans who did not know the British well enough to realize this was not an end of the matter. The Redcoats commenced the next phase by attending to the marksmen concealed in the houses of Charlestown. This they did with artillery fire from the fort at Copp's Hill on the Boston side of the harbor, using a special cannon ball called a carcass. This had gunpowder in it that burned while the ball was in flight and continued to do so after it struck. When a few dozen of these crashed into the wooden houses of the town, they were ablaze. At the same time, British marines with torches set fire to the edges of the town. The American marksmen, smoked out, departed on the double and joined the forces in the redoubt.

To see that the men in the fortification received no reinforcements, food, or water, all of which were acutely needed, the British warships kept up steady gunfire on Charlestown Neck, the low narrow land across which supplies and men must come. Then the troops lined up for another charge up the slopes.

In this second advance up Breed's Hill were the remnants of the regiments which had taken such cruel punishment in the first charge as well as new regiments brought up as replacements. On they came, as before, in the same perfect order, beautiful straight lines, shining brass, brilliant uniforms, the officers in outfits bought in London at prices that would purchase a farm in New England.

Why the British ordered another advance up that bloody slope in the face of the deadly gunfire of men behind earthen walls that even their cannon balls could not damage is a mystery to anyone until he takes time to study the English character. An Englishman's idea of honor was to do things the hardest and most dangerous way. They could have cut off the entire American force by a landing at Charlestown Neck, covered by the guns of their men-of-war. Then they could have starved out the Minutemen in the redoubt.

But the British had been challenged and then beaten by a crowd of colonial country clowns. Any King's officer would have bet a golden guinea this mob of Americans would have run at the sound of artillery fire and the sight of the long, steady line of bayonets advancing toward them. Their attack had failed miserably, and life would not have been worth living to most of these British officers if the matter had rested there. So on this second charge, a very foolish maneuver, rode the honor of every officer in General Gage's army. And they could give this second order to advance because of British bravery and discipline.

The Americans, although largely of English ancestry, were not the same kind of men. Too long had they lived the free, self-reliant and independent life of this land of frontiers to be able to take an order unquestioningly. Every man in the ranks considered he was a pretty good officer himself. If the men thought an order was sensible, there were no better soldiers. If they thought the order was foolish, whoever gave the command suddenly discovered he had no troops. No officer could ever have marched American troops up Breed's Hill a second time, not in close formation.

However, it was the British who were attacking, and on they came, just as bright and beautiful as before in the June sunshine and just as steady. They reached a point, an order was barked out, and the horrible crash of the volley from the Breed's Hill redoubt rolled out. There followed the smoke, shouts, and cries of agony. After reloading, more shots roared from behind the ramparts. Then the remnants of the Redcoat regiments straggled away, some walking, some limping, some crawling, a few running. On the ground lay more bodies, some moving, most of them still.

By this time the condition of the American troops in the redoubt had deteriorated. They had worked hard all night with no sleep. Their food was gone and so was their water. It was a hot day and there was no breeze inside the fortification. Powder and ball were very low, with no more than two rounds left for some of the men.

A few had lost their fighting spirit, grumbling because reinforcements and supplies had not arrived. There were mutterings of treachery in the high command, talk that these regiments were being sacrificed. A few sneaked away on the pretense of helping wounded to the rear, but nearly every man stayed, and the casualties had been negligible.

Then a battery of British six-pounder field artillery down by the beach began to fire. This was the first near-at-hand cannon fire, for this battery had at first been supplied with the wrong-sized balls. They began to knock the top off the American ramparts, showering the men inside with dirt and stones. After considerable artillery fire the third British advance began with drums pounding and fifes squealing. The regiments which had taken such fearful losses marched up this same slope, past the bodies of fallen comrades strewn everywhere.

No other army in the world could have advanced after those two terrible close-range massacres in front of the American fort. They needed iron discipline and bravery, and they had it. Those of the officers who had survived the first two charges led their men, risking death. This time English persistence won. American bullets mowed down many Redcoats, but ammunition was short and there was not enough gunfire to halt the straight red line of men.

They came steadily on, over the walls of the redoubt. With their wicked bayonets they charged down into the midst of the Americans. The Minutemen fought back with the few bayonets they had and with rocks and musket butts, but it was a losing fight and they edged back, never giving way to panic.

This is the stage of the battle where the Americans took heavy losses. Doctor Joseph Warren was there, fighting as a private, although he was a colonel. He had come over to Charlestown to fight because he wanted to be in this battle and he fought like a lion, rallying the men as they retreated. As the Americans withdrew from the fort, a British musket ball caught Dr. Warren behind the ear and he was instantly killed.

Grapeshot from the British battery of six-pounders cut up the Americans as they retreated into the open ground behind the redoubt on Breed's Hill. The casualties would have been much worse had it not been for Christian Febiger, a Danish officer fighting on the side of the American colonists. He led some of the American troops who were on nearby Bunker Hill against the British just in time to check their pursuit of the fleeing garrison of the Breed's Hill redoubt. They had plenty of ammunition, and the British feared a trap in the gathering twilight, so the Minutemen escaped over the neck to the mainland.

The battle was ended. The King's troops had the hill and they had Charlestown. The Minutemen retreated no further than Prospect Hill on the mainland, where they received food, water, ammunition and reinforcements. There they dug in, building another redoubt and ready for another fight as soon as the Redcoats cared to march against their earthworks.

The British never attacked Prospect Hill. General Howe had Breed's Hill and Bunker Hill and he had his honor. He also had an army that was practically a wreck, with a thousand casualties. British burial parties, stretcher-bearers and surgeons took over the battlefield as darkness fell. The Redcoats who were still unwounded lay down wherever they were, completely exhausted.

The British won this fight that has ever since been called the Battle of Bunker Hill. But there was still a ring around Boston, a ring now made of harder stuff because the men who constituted it had learned a great deal on that seventeenth of June. Inside the ring lay a British army still be-

sieged, weary and weak from one of the toughest battles English troops had ever fought. The men and officers no longer
talked of the American army, or thought of it, as if it were a
rabble of noisy and cowardly bumpkins. The British now were
really afraid of the men who had inflicted such disastrous
losses upon them. This fear was to persist throughout the
long War for Independence wherever there was a British
officer or men who had been in the dreadful carnage at Bunker
Hill.

5 ⌒

Bungle at Bunker Hill

IT NEVER WAS DIFFICULT for the general of the American patriot army besieging Boston to find out what General Gage and his Redcoats were doing or planning to do. Boston was a town of spies.

Therefore, when the British high command evolved a plan to break the ring of American troops that held Boston in a viselike grip, General Artemas Ward at his Cambridge headquarters soon knew of it. They intended to occupy Charlestown, then move on Cambridge, roll up the American line and break the siege. Were the British regulars really successful in their attack on the little trained and inexperienced militia, the American army would be destroyed and this rebellion would be over.

General Ward and his staff weighed carefully the information. Beside Gage there were other able English generals across the river—Howe, Clinton, Burgoyne. Were they capable of planting this information and then, after the strength of the American army shifted to Charlestown to meet the attack, might they come pouring in from the opposite direction, by way of Roxbury? If they decoyed the Americans into

Charlestown, then threw their strength into Cambridge from the Roxbury direction, there would be a massive British victory, an end to the colonial army.

So General Ward sent a limited force to Charlestown to build a fort he hoped would contain the British regulars and, if it did not, then at least slow them up enough so their intentions would be clear. Then there would be time for the American army to retreat and avoid disaster. He did not commit his main forces. The spies in Boston had been correct, it turned out, as the events of June 17, 1775, unfolded. The British attack was at Charlestown; the Roxbury front was quiet and nothing was to be feared from that quarter.

Furthermore, news reaching American headquarters clearly indicated to General Ward that the British attack was not going well. Ward knew the regiments he had sent must be hard pressed. All night they had labored, digging earth for the fort; they had fought the Redcoats to a standstill, and they were probably short of powder and ball.

Good generalship requires that the regiments strike the enemy at the right time and place. Now, in this afternoon of June 17, was the time to send fresh troops from his main forces into the battle to support the tired Americans against the even more fatigued British. General Ward ordered Major Scarborough Gridley forward to Charlestown with his artillery and he ordered Colonel John Mansfield to lead his 19th Regiment of infantry to join the garrison at Bunker Hill. These were excellent decisions.

Off went Mansfield's regiment, fresh men who had enjoyed a good night's sleep and a restful morning. They had food, water, powder and ball and plenty of energy. These were Essex County men, companies from Salem, Beverly and Manchester, companies from Lynn, Danvers and Ipswich, men who had the patriot cause very much at heart.

Major Gridley and his horse artillery were ahead of them on the way to Charlestown. Then, at Cobble Hill, a short distance before reaching Charlestown Neck, something happened. Gridley started to think. The result of his thoughts produced certain conclusions. First, he decided the American regiments in Charlestown could not hold out and must soon retreat. Second, he decided he must engage the British men-of-war then bombarding Charlestown Neck and sweeping it with cannon balls from their batteries. So he halted his battery, unlimbered and commenced firing at the enemy ships.

Here was something that happened mainly because the American force was not yet really an army, but a collection of military units raised in the various towns and accustomed to acting independently for well over a century. Gridley had orders from headquarters, the orders of the commanding general, yet it seemed not at all strange to him that on the way to the battlefield he should disregard the orders and do as he thought best.

This was a new army. The idea of a chain of command had not really implanted itself. The concept of an army of which the maneuvers were controlled by a supreme commander was wholly strange to men who knew only their local officers. General Ward thought Gridley's battery was soon to be at Breed's Hill, joining the battle. Actually it was far to the rear, at Cobble Hill, doing what Major Gridley had decided was more important.

Gridley had not been at Cobble Hill for long when Colonel Mansfield's regiment appeared, swinging along toward the firing on Breed's Hill in Charlestown. Major Gridley rode up to the colonel and told him he was taking this position with his battery to cover the retreat. He ordered Mansfield to halt here with his infantry and support the artillery.

Probably there is no schoolboy today who would not at once ask how a major could order a colonel to do anything. Yet so new was this army of American units, each from its own town, that there was lacking in Colonel Mansfield's mind any idea that Gridley was acting strangely and in a most unmilitary manner.

Colonel Mansfield apparently thought Gridley was correct. Disregarding the orders to march his regiment to the battle in Charlestown, he halted his men and gave orders to take positions in support of this battery of guns. It was at about this time in the afternoon, while Mansfield's regiment halted within sight of the battle, that the third British attack started, came up the slope and overwhelmed the defenders of the Breed's Hill redoubt.

The Americans were short of powder and ball. They fired what they had, then they fought with rocks and musket butts, finally retreating in disorder that nearly became a rout. Had Mansfield's regiment, with plenty of powder and ball, been behind those ramparts, the third advance of the Redcoats probably would have ended in disaster for them. As it was, Mansfield's regiment was at Cobble Hill to cover the retreat, and the exhausted troops of the King's army did not care to invite another battle with fresh troops on this disastrous day.

The battle ended at sundown and Colonel Mansfield's regiment remained all night at Winter Hill, just beyond Charlestown Neck, ready to meet any British attempt to advance. There was no such attempt; the British were too busy with their dead and wounded.

Apparently there was no move made at American headquarters to discover why Major Gridley and Colonel Mansfield had done as they did. To examine the conduct of a battle was probably another of many things this new army had not got around to providing for. Indeed, so makeshift were communications and the staff and means of transmitting messages that it is possible General Ward actually did not know what Gridley and Mansfield had done.

However, the organization of the American army was progressing. In July, General Ward was relieved by General George Washington, a thorough military man. At once things began to tighten up. Colonel Mansfield appeared to be in excellent standing under the new commander in chief. Several times he was officer of the day.

It was in August that three of the officers of Mansfield's regiment went to General Washington and accused their colonel of cowardice on the day of Bunker Hill and gave the particulars of what took place at Cobble Hill. In the regiment there had been a good deal of feuding and bad feeling, and it may be the three officers made their charges as a result of this. Or they may have been conscientious men who did this from a sense of duty. Washington could not ignore these grave charges, and he ordered a trial before a court-martial of thirteen officers.

In September the trial was held, and the court-martial rendered a verdict that Colonel John Mansfield was guilty of "backwardness" in the execution of his duty. The court did not find him guilty of cowardice. Mansfield was "cashiered"; that is, he was deprived of his rank of colonel. Further than that, the court ruled that he was unfit to serve in the army.

This was, of course, a crushing verdict, the severity of which was probably due to the new discipline brought to the army by General Washington. It is likely that Mansfield's blunder in obeying the order of Gridley, his inferior officer, had not seemed a grievous offense to American headquarters on June seventeenth.

The Americans had little experience in running an army. In the French and Indian War the American companies and battalions and regiments fought well, yet the high command and the staff were British. When a British staff officer arrived with an order for an American colonial unit, the authority of the order was at once recognized. The staff officer was a King's officer.

But it took time for the idea to take root that an American general had supreme authority. This idea had not prevailed in Colonel Mansfield's mind on June seventeenth. Subconsciously he felt that decisions were for him to make and General Ward's order was something he had a right to reconsider.

The verdict against Colonel Mansfield was part of the procedure of learning to become an army. No longer were colonels, or privates, to consider their judgment to be as good as that of the general of the army. Perhaps there would have been no Revolution were it not for this habit of thought. Americans still feel that way. That is one of the things that characterizes them as Americans. But long since they have learned to take orders, and the trial of Colonel Mansfield, so soon after Washington's arrival, may be one of the fundamental steps in our military history.

So this good man yielded the command of the regiment he had helped to build from the sturdy men of Essex County and he returned to his native Lynn. There his fellow townsmen were completely unable to understand the decision of the court-martial. An independent lot then, and in later years as well, the Lynners felt their beloved John Mansfield had been victimized because of an error in judgment made in the heat of battle.

The colonel felt his disgrace keenly, yet his spirits must have risen as he gradually came to realize the feelings of the Lynners toward him. Their views they expressed in what they did. They elected him to the Committee of Correspondence, Inspection and Safety, an important post in Revolutionary America. He was elected on several occasions to the post of town moderator. This was, and still is, an important position in the New England town-meeting form of government.

However grieved John Mansfield may have felt at the way the army dealt with him, his zeal for the cause of independence abated not at all. He worked hard to raise men for the army and served faithfully on the Committee of Correspondence. A man of different character might have considered communicating with the British, as did Benedict Arnold. Or he might have joined the Tory forces.

Mansfield was as faithful in Lynn, shorn of all rank, as he had been when he had led his regiment. He lived to see war's end and the formation of a new nation, the United States of America. He lived many years after that, respected by everyone in the little farming and shoemaking town of Lynn, sought out when an important post was to be filled and sympathized with whenever in shoeshop or tavern or in Market Square there was a discussion of the part the 19th Regiment of Essex County men played on that seventeenth of June.

Long after the war, when he was in his eighties, his end came. They laid him away under the elms of Lynn's Western Burying Ground, surrounded by the gravestones of his family and his friends and many of the men who had fought in the French and Indian War and in our War for Independence.

6

The Guns of Ticonderoga

AFTER THE GHASTLY LOSSES the British army suffered at the battle of Bunker Hill in Charlestown in its effort to break the ring of American troops besieging Boston, no further attempts were made against the earthworks the colonial troops had built on every side. The English high command simply did not dare to mount an attack on fortifications held by these American militiamen who had such deadly aim with their muskets.

The Americans were now commanded by General Washington, a man of military experience and profound wisdom in the art of war. He knew better than to throw his troops against the earthworks the British enemy had erected all the way around the town of Boston. To attack without the support of artillery to break the fortifications he well knew could result in a bloody reverse that might wreck the morale of his army.

Month after month of the siege of Boston went by with no important action by either side. Washington did not permit time to be wasted, however. He used this lull to teach his mob of patriot soldiers something of military discipline and order.

62

These men, independent of mind and a rough and ready lot, did not take much more kindly to obeying the orders of their own officers than they did to obeying the laws of the Parliament in London. As for their living quarters, a disorderly collection of shacks grew up, built every which way.

General Washington gradually changed all this. As time went on, orders were obeyed, drunken men fetched up in the guardhouse; the camp was rearranged so that tents and barracks were laid out in straight lines, and rules about digging latrines and burying garbage were strictly enforced. The encampment of the American army began to look better, behave better and smell better.

While working to make this vast aggregation of local militia companies into an army, General Washington never for a moment lost sight of the fact that stalemates do not win campaigns. The objective of this campaign was to capture Boston, surrounded by strong field fortifications and garrisoned by excellent British troops, a fine army even after the casualties at Bunker Hill. Never could this be done until he acquired artillery more powerful than the little four-pounders such as Gridley had commanded on the day of Bunker Hill.

Where to get artillery appeared to be the question without an answer until the day when Ethan Allen and his Vermonters, the "Green Mountain boys," came out of the forests at the southern end of Lake Champlain to surprise and capture Fort Ticonderoga. One of the most important fortresses in North America, built by the French to command the entire Champlain and Hudson River area, it had fallen to the English in the French and Indian War.

Now a seat of British military power, Fort Ticonderoga was a treasure house of the materials of war: gunpowder, rations, muskets and, most important, cannon. Here were huge eighteen- and twenty-four-pounders and mortars to fire a projectile in a high trajectory that would come crashing down from the sky into an enemy position. Ethan Allen and his Green Mountain boys had deserved well of their country when they surprised and stormed Ticonderoga.

When the word of the capture reached Washington at his Cambridge headquarters, one thought immediately leaped to the forefront of his mind. Those cannon, here in his lines, would blast a wide gap in the enemy's field fortifications, a gap through which would pour the American regiments. But the guns were at Ticonderoga, three hundred miles away. There was no way they could be loaded aboard ships and brought to Washington at Cambridge. They must come over narrow, muddy roads, many of them through the wilderness with steep grades and sharp curves.

At the time of the siege of Boston this was a task for oxen or horses, taking weeks of a plodding, backbreaking journey. And whoever was in charge needed to be a man of vigor and resourcefulness. No man ever becomes a great general unless he has the gift of picking leaders. George Washington, of course, had that gift, and here was one of the instances where he demonstrated it. He selected Colonel Henry Knox to see to it that the guns of Ticonderoga were brought to the siege of Boston.

Knox, an excellent artilleryman, had not long before been the proprietor of a bookstore in Boston. Along with an interest in books he had an insatiable interest in things military. In his Boston store he studied every book on guns, fortifications, strategy and the use of artillery that he imported from Europe for sale to officers of the British regiments which gar-

risoned the town. When the time came that it was advisable
for those who favored the Patriot cause to get out of town in
a hurry, Henry Knox was one of those who got over to the
other side of the Charles River as fast as his legs would carry
him.

It did not take the command of the new army long to discover that here was a man of considerable capabilities, so he
advanced rapidly. Until the capture of Ticonderoga he had
been commander of the army's artillery, yet with no guns except a few light four-pounders. So when Washington sent him
to get these captured cannon, he was giving him the opportunity to provide his branch of the service with the weapons
it now almost entirely lacked. If he succeeded, he would command a force of great strength and importance. If he failed, he
would continue to command units that were artillery only in
name, a position that verged on the ludicrous.

Knox was a huge man with round red cheeks, a head shaped
like one of his own cannon balls and a great supply of driving
energy. Once he had his orders from General Washington, he
selected men, started them for Lake Champlain and then himself set forth by way of New York, planning and organizing.

Reaching Ticonderoga in early December, his men were at
once set to work getting the guns onto sledges, and the draft
animals, horses and oxen Colonel Knox had assembled from
the surrounding countryside, were made ready. Out from the
fort came the guns, each hauled by two yoke of oxen or two
pairs of horses.

Down to the shore of Lake George they plodded, where
waited flat-bottomed bateaux which Knox had rounded up
from various points on the lake. He hoped to accomplish
thirty miles of the long journey by using water transport,

which is generally much easier.

The passage of Lake George was difficult. The wind was ahead, so these big flat-bottomed craft moved only when the men took to the sweeps and rowed the heavy cargoes southward. One bateau commenced to leak and settle. Fortunately the commander realized she was not going to be afloat for long, so he managed to get his vessel into shallow water before she sank.

The men took out the cannon, bailed out the bateau, raised her, calked her and continued on toward the south end of the lake with their cargo of heavy guns. Next came a phase when oxen and horses and hard-bitten drivers were important, as the long line of vehicles wound over the road to Albany.

People came out of the farmhouses along the way to stare at the longest procession of animals and sledges they had ever seen go over that road. These people knew the importance of the guns and where they were bound; they cheered and brought good food for the men and feed for the animals.

When the long convoy of eighty guns reached Albany, a new kind of difficulty confronted Colonel Henry Knox. The weather was balmy and warm with a December thaw, so the ice over the Hudson River was not strong enough to bear the weight of these heavy cannon. The men chopped holes in the ice, bailed out water and spread it so it would freeze during the night and strengthen the ice. This helped a little, and a couple of colder nights did more to strengthen the ice. With a fresh snowfall to cover the roads so the sledges could travel, it seemed to Colonel Knox and General Schuyler of Albany that it was safe to go forward.

The crossing of the Hudson River was a success until near the end. Over ice that rumbled and made cracking noises the oxen and horses and the heavy sledges made their way, one at a time. One of the last pieces to cross was a fine long-barreled eighteen-pounder, a gun designed to throw a heavy ball a long distance.

All went well until near the far bank of the river. Then the noises of the ice grew louder and the gun and its horse-drawn sled began to go down. The driver cut the traces, whipped up his horses, and they galloped for the shore. Into the Hudson River went the gun.

It was there, around the dismal hole in the ice where this weapon for General Washington had disappeared, that Colonel Henry Knox saw the spirit of the Albany people. When they pitched in immediately to help, it was clear this was not a Boston war or a Massachusetts war; it was an American war. To learn this was, to Colonel Knox, almost compensation for his misfortunes.

The Albany folks rigged a tripod of heavy timbers over the hole in the ice. They located a big block, rove a line through it, and then a couple of men started fishing around on the bottom of the river. Somehow they managed to get a line under the gun forward and another aft by patiently working with weighted and looped ropes for over an hour.

Word was passed to a crowd of men ashore who had the other end of the lines. They gave a great shout and walked away with the line, putting their backs into it. Up from the depths came the eighteen-pounder and the sled to which it was lashed, like a bucket out of a well. From the shore a great cheer went up as the line was slipped off the gun and made fast to the sled. At another command the gang of men ashore walked the line, the sled commenced to move, and away it went across the ice and up onto land.

Then there occurred an incident that showed why Henry Knox, the colonel who had once sold books in his Boston store, could get men to do things he wanted done. He clambered up onto the gun, raised his hand for silence and bellowed in a voice that could be heard up and down the shore:

"You men of Albany have saved this valuable cannon for our cause. It is my order that from this moment its name is *Albany.*"

Down from the cannon came Knox, as cheers rose from the crowd. He snapped out the order to advance, the men yelled at their horses and oxen, long whips cracked, the oxgoads were busy, and the artillery began to move down the Post Road. Three hundred draft animals, eighty sledges, a gang of New York drivers and some men from the Boston army moved along the highway, with Knox urging them on. He kept at his men with a word here and a word there all through that winter afternoon until he could tell by the way his men and his animals acted that it was time to halt, build fires, feed and bed down for the night. When the column stopped, the last of an old-rose winter sunset was long gone.

In the cold dawn the guns began to move again, through the valley of the Hudson toward Kinderhook. Knox was up and down the column, a sharp eye on everything, with now and then a good word for this or that man that gave fresh will to go forward.

The line of heavy sledges, each drawn by two or four or six horses or oxen, with the guns lashed down and covered by protecting tarpaulins, reached as far as the eye could see, along the flat, up the rise, over the crest and out of sight. The animals and men and sledges were black against the snow. The breath from the nostrils of the beasts left a white vapor in the cold air.

Here and there along the valley road stood farmhouses, and generally from each one a man came out with an enormous forkful of hay to toss onto one of the sledges. Then the farmer would scurry back to his barn for another forkful to put on a sledge further down the line when it reached his driveway. And the lady of the house trotted out with food to hand to one of the men and then back into the house for another plateful. Knox's company had a particularly good opportunity to judge the cakemaking capabilities of the women of the valley.

Colonel Knox, all two hundred and eighty pounds of him, was always at the spot where any difficulty arose. A broken runner, a lame animal, a driver who had lost his courage and wished to return to Albany—whatever the problem, he was there at once to solve it. It was Henry Knox, his spirit, his presence, his way of finding a workable answer to whatever went wrong, that kept the column moving onward toward Boston.

The easy going ended when they left the Hudson River valley at Kinderhook to head east. Now the road had steeper grades and the small hill farms were farther apart, although the column still received presents of hay and food, for these people, too, knew what this long procession of heavy loads meant.

Beyond this region of hill farms lay the forests of the Berkshires, traversed by a trail termed a "post road"—steep pitches with shaky bridges over mountain streams. Most of these bridges had to be shored up with timber which the men cut from the forests crowding down to the roadside before it was safe to take the heavy loads across.

It is doubtful if wheeled vehicles could ever have carried such weights over those steep, narrow and rocky roads. It was easier to handle the heavy loads on runners than on wheels. There was no mud to trap the wheels; it had frozen solid, and the runners passed along much more smoothly. Colonel Knox was leading his column through this rugged terrain at just the right time of year.

In the wild and tumbled hills of the Berkshires lies a long stretch of spruce, pine and hemlock called the Evergreens, and this primitive, unpopulated region was the hardest going of all. When a sledge broke down, it had to be repaired with wood cut at the side of the road. On those steep pitches there were often twenty men pulling on the drag ropes to help the animals. Sometimes they took the oxen off the sledge behind and doubled up the hill with eight or ten draft animals.

Going downhill was more of a problem, for if one of the sledges got loose, it would take animals and men with it and pile up in a gorge at the bottom with the bodies under it. To control the loads on the downgrade, the drivers made fast a tackle to a big tree at the crest and paid out the rope gradually.

It was bitterly cold in the Berkshires in December. The animals were bedded down in one group, snugged up to each other so they could share the warmth of their bodies. The men slept the same way, with good fires of dry wood going all night. The hay stored on the sledges was doled out carefully to the oxen and horses, for in this forest country there was no way of replenishing it. Rations for the men were issued carefully, and this vigorous crew was ravenously hungry. No good ladies came out to the roadside with cakes

the fire, and it looked to everyone on both sides as if this bombardment would be followed by an American infantry attack.

However, not all the new cannon were taking part in this bombardment; the best of them were in concealment. Days later, in March, the order came, and the guns started rolling. Out through Roxbury they went in the small hours of a black night and on toward Dorchester Heights.

This was like the night on Bunker Hill; hundreds of men in the inky blackness, digging. They worked away, dark shapes looming, shovels and picks making little sounds as they bit into the gravel, low-voiced commands, no lights. The drivers with the big guns stayed well back so as to keep out of the way while more men came up the slope and went to work, silent shadows in the darkness, appearing suddenly, then fading.

As the men worked, they heard the booming of the guns over on the north side of Boston as the American artillery at Lechmere and Cobble Hill fired at the British fieldworks and the British fired back. The sky flickered with the flashes of this duel; everyone in Boston was watching, including the British, awaiting the American assault in the morning.

It was in the small hours of morning that the guns were ordered up to the emplacements these laboring hundreds had built. Colonel Knox marked out the site of each piece; they rumbled into their places, and by dawn all of the big guns brought over the snow from Ticonderoga were in position so they covered the town of Boston and the British ships in the harbor.

The King's ships moved into position to bombard this fort the rebels had built during one night, like the redoubt on

Bunker Hill back in June, nine months before. The English ships blazed away, but they scored no hits. They could not elevate their guns sufficiently to reach the American position on Dorchester Heights. The Americans fired but little. Gunpowder they had, yet not enough to afford wastefulness. However, they did fire enough so the Royal Navy could see the reach of the new guns. A few splashes close aboard were enough.

The British then prepared to mount an infantry attack against this American fort that now commanded Boston and the main ship channel into the harbor as well. Their luck was bad, however. A storm was brewing, and the next day a real northeaster struck with driving rain and gale winds that blew two of their transports hard aground. Two days passed before the British were able to get their stranded vessels off into good water. This interval provided the British high command time in which to do some serious thinking.

No longer did they believe a good cannonade and the sight of the long lines of Redcoats coming were enough to make American soldiers run. The thought of attacking American troops who were dug in, after Bunker Hill, was enough to give any English officer a cold chill.

It really can be said that the lost battle of Bunker Hill resulted in victory at Dorchester Heights. The capabilities shown by American troops at the former engagement made the British generals appreciate the folly of attacking this new fort, particularly when it had artillery capable of sweeping attacking troops with grapeshot and guns with a range to put solid shot into any British man-of-war entering or leaving Boston.

So it turned out Colonel Knox was not obliged to fire

eighteen- and twenty-four-pound shot into his beloved Boston. The order from General Washington was to wait. At last, in the evening of March 16, 1776, there was evidence the British high command had reached a decision. Word came that the King's troops were to evacuate Boston in the morning.

This they did. The ships, crowded with troops, sailed down the harbor within easy reach of the long guns on Dorchester Heights. The guns were silent. Henry Knox and his men watched until the ships were hull down on the horizon. They knew that by now the American troops would be marching into Boston town. There would be celebrating aplenty and a high time in the old town this night. They were willing to miss it. The big guns they had brought from so far away, giving everything they had to keep them moving, meant more to them. Now their tortuous journey from Ticonderoga over the mountains and across the snows was bearing fruit; the last of the King's ships were sailing over the rim of the eastern horizon.

It meant to every man on the Heights that this was their country now, all theirs, without one Redcoat or royal official from the eastern provinces of Maine to Boston, from Boston to New York, from Boston to beyond those Berkshire hills where they had hauled these beautiful guns through the forests, up the hills, down the steep pitches and across shaky bridges.

Yet every man knew in his heart that a long road and many battles lay ahead before there could be peace for them to make something of their new country. The British fleet had carried the army away to the eastward, probably to Halifax. They would return some day, everyone knew. Where would they land?

Rifleman Murphy

TIMOTHY MURPHY had decided he needed a new gun. That is why he set out that morning from Mr. Van Campen's farm in Wyoming, Pennsylvania, to tramp down to Easton to see Jim Golcher, the gunsmith. It was a long journey on foot. Wyoming lay on the western fringe of the settlements in 1775, about halfway between Philadelphia, an old and long-established town where people wore good clothes and considered an Indian a curiosity, and Pittsburgh, which was a fort in the wilderness where a man who ventured very far from the log palisades risked fetching up as a corpse, with his scalp a trophy hanging from some Indian's belt.

Wyoming was worth fighting for, Timothy Murphy had concluded. Lying in the Susquehanna Valley, it was a place of rich farming land, while in its hills lay coal and iron that some day would be the making of an iron industry. The men of Wyoming were willing to fight, which was well. Like the Belgae, whom Caesar described, they were engaged in almost daily battle. The Indians were in the forest just beyond the fields of this frontier town, always ready to attack a settler, take his scalp and be gone, or perhaps to raid his house and carry his wife and children into captivity.

In spite of scalpings and burnings the men of Wyoming managed to hang onto their frontier farms at the edge of the dark forest that was home for the many Indians. That they had managed to survive, work their farms, cut down more trees each year to enlarge their farms was due not only to their tremendous courage but to the guns they carried, the Pennsylvania rifles.

It was good fortune that at this time, when settlers were pushing westward into lands where the Indians were numerous and merciless, the settlers had this weapon so superior to anything the Indians had. The British regulars had nothing like it either. The brown Bess smoothbore musket issued to the King's troops fired a bullet on so wobbly and inaccurate a course that a hit at seventy yards was only luck. With a Pennsylvania rifle it was possible to break a teacup at two hundred yards. In Easton were a half-dozen gunsmiths who could make these weapons; other such craftsmen worked in Allentown and three dozen of them in Lancaster. Mostly Germans, they were of that breed known as "Pennsylvania Dutchmen," a race as famous as the Yankees themselves.

Murphy had a Pennsylvania rifle. It was a good one, and he knew how to use it. Anyone in Wyoming who entered into a shooting match with him always had to pay. But thoughtful, black-haired Tim Murphy had been turning things over in his mind. Stocky and strong, he was nevertheless very fast on his feet, and well for him that he was, for no more than a week ago a party of six Indians had glided out of the forest and started for him as he worked in the field. His rifle was at hand. He leveled it and dropped the leading Indian at better than two hundred yards, but this is a distance an

Indian can cover in an amazingly short time—far less time then it takes to load a rifle.

So Tim Murphy ran for it. He was swift, outraced them and escaped. That was the day Tim decided he must see Jim Golcher, the gunsmith of Easton. All of his savings were in his pocket, along with what he could borrow from Mr. Van Campen. This was for a new gun. He intended to have Jim Golcher make him a double-barreled rifle. To be sure, he had been fast enough to outrun those Indians. But what if he had tripped and fallen? Timothy Murphy felt of his mop of black hair. Had he stumbled as he ran, his scalp would be a trophy hanging at an Indian's belt. Tim grinned; he was vain enough to think it would make an unusually handsome prize.

When Tim got to Easton, Golcher listened carefully to the plan for a double-barreled rifle, and his eyes shone.

"It will be difficult, my boy," he said, "but it can be done. I will start right now. You find yourself lodgings. And be patient."

Tim paid Golcher his assortment of coins and went strolling off to see the sights of the town. He had time to linger in taverns and on street corners, listening to the talk. That in itself was a wonderful experience. In Wyoming when neighbors met they might talk of weather, crops, horses or pigs or cattle and always Indians. No conversation in Wyoming ever ended without some talk about what the Indians had done or might do.

But here were people who had recently been in Philadelphia; there was one who had a brother in New York who could write, and another had talked with a mariner from the crew of a Boston vessel. Tim Murphy could not read, but in the tavern a man read from a newspaper twice every day while everybody in the place crowded close to listen. So Tim learned a lot about what was going on in that part of America which lay beyond the farms and forests of Wyoming, Pennsylvania.

Boston was the place to watch, everyone agreed; Boston with its huge garrison of British regulars which every so often went on a march in regimental strength through the countryside looking for military supplies the people up that way had stored out of sight. Timothy Murphy heard about the British expedition from Boston to nearby Salem, how the townspeople had thwarted the Redcoats, how every town in those regions had its company of soldiers—Minutemen, they called them—and he heard how that day these Minutemen had come down all the roads leading into Salem to face the King's soldiers. Not a shot fired at Salem, yet everyone seemed to think lead would be flying before very long.

Tim got his new double-barreled rifle, tested it and was deeply gratified. Golcher gave him his blessing.

"Young fellow, all I've got to say is I'd like to be there to watch them Indians when you fire this second barrel. They'll think you've got medicine made by the Old Harry himself. Good luck."

Tim's eyes lighted up as he shook hands with the gunsmith and started his long westward journey to the Wyoming settlement on the Susquehanna. His pocket was empty, but he did not mind. He was thinking of the time to come when the Indians might rush him after he had fired his first shot.

His pocket did not remain empty for long. On a village green in a town a day's march to the west they were having a shooting contest. On a handkerchief lay some coins, the prize for the winning rifleman. On a tree a hundred paces distant a small paper was nailed. Timothy Murphy asked to be allowed to compete, and they told him to stand up when all the others had fired.

"I'll use my rifle as a hammer on yonder nail that holds the paper to the tree," he announced with a broad Irish grin.

Carefully he sighted on the paper already well perforated with bullet holes by the town's riflemen. Tim squeezed the trigger; his rifle spat fire, the powder smoke drifted down wind and the piece of paper fluttered to the ground. Racing to the tree, the committee in charge of the contest carefully examined the results of this last shot. They dug into the tree with their long knives; at last they recovered the nail.

Timothy Murphy's bullet, striking the nail on the head as he had said it would, had driven it deep into the trunk of the tree. The little collection of coins was his prize. Everyone crowded around to shake hands with him, and a supper and a night's lodging were part of his reward. In the morning he continued on his journey back to Wyoming.

There is no record of whether any Indians slipped out of the forest to attack Timothy Murphy as he went about his work in the rich Susquehanna Valley in that spring of 1775, so we do not know if his two-barreled rifle taught the savages of the forest the lesson he had in mind for them. And it was only during that spring that he was on the frontier of civilization at these rich Susquehanna Valley lands. By the time summer came Tim had left the valley to go on a long journey.

It was on April 19, 1775, that the shots everyone had been expecting were fired. The news of Concord and Lexington spread slowly over America's thirteen colonies, as this was before the day of the telegraph, yet no news had ever had such impact on the American people. This was war, total war. With an astonishing oneness of mind the American people went about the business of seeing to it that this country they had hewn out of the wilderness was to be theirs.

The news reached Timothy Murphy out at Wyoming, Pennsylvania, on one of America's western frontiers. Not long afterward he learned that a new military organization was being formed by Colonel William Thompson—the Riflemen of Pennsylvania. Murphy needed no more than to hear the name to know that he belonged in this regiment. With some reluctance he left the frontier at Wyoming, where the struggle with the Indian tribes was an issue very much alive.

Yet this war with the British seemed to Murphy to be much the bigger thing. Added to his knowledge of England's tyrannical treatment of the colonies was his Irish inheritance that taught him British oppression must always be resisted. He slung his double-barreled rifle over his shoulder, set forth for Northumberland and on June 29 he was enlisted in Captain Lowdon's company of riflemen.

The Riflemen of Pennsylvania soon started off for the war. That meant Boston. There the British army was, in the town surrounded by an army of American militia that formed a ring around the place. The Pennsylvanians marched to strengthen the siege army of General Washington, the newly appointed commander.

To say that these men marched is not quite accurate. They had never been drilled, as had the Massachusetts troops and the Maryland and other outfits from well-populated areas. They were frontiersmen, people who always had made their own decisions, in a country where every man had to take care of himself or die. Marching to them seemed ridiculous;

they walked when they wished to get somewhere, walked with long strides all day at a pace that would leave town-bred soldiers exhausted.

Uniforms were unknown with them. They wore the clothes of the frontier—fringed buckskin jackets, moccasins, coonskin hats, leather bags for provisions. And every man had slung on his shoulder his long rifle, accurate at two hundred yards, effective at three hundred and very useful at greater ranges. Unused to discipline, they were a turbulent lot.

When they reached New York, they were told considerable information about a certain well-known Tory. These Pennsylvanians were quite unable to see why such a reprobate was allowed to live unmolested, so they went to his house to deal with him according to their ideas. Fortunately for the Tory, he received word the Riflemen were on their way to call on him, so he was out of the house and over the back fence before they arrived. The Riflemen went through his house from top to bottom, helped themselves to anything they thought useful or interesting and went on their way toward the siege of Boston.

In Hartford, Connecticut, another Tory was not as fortunate in receiving word that the Pennsylvanians were on their way to see him. They caught him and promptly treated him to the old-fashioned ritual of tarring and feathering. When they reached Cambridge, the headquarters of the American army besieging Boston, there was a rough time trying to make soldiers of them. Ordinary military chores, such as every man who was ever in the army can recall, simply made these frontiersmen laugh. They had never heard of "policing the area" by picking up debris, or burying garbage or digging trenches or making forts. They declined such duties.

Of course, some of them got drunk and made a commotion. When the disorderly ones were collared and tossed into the guardhouse, which was another army institution with which they were quite unfamiliar, the rest of the regiment were deeply insulted. Quickly getting together, they marched on the guardhouse, seized the guards and took the place apart.

That General Washington could handle these wild men who had always lived beyond civilization, its customs and its laws is one of the instances of his great capability for handling men and uniting them for the great purpose of this war. Washington planned an exhibition at which the entire army drew up on both sides of a shooting field to watch the fourteen hundred Pennsylvania Riflemen fire at a target two hundred yards distant. The target was an upright log seven inches in diameter. The Riflemen made the splinters fly and finally the log, so shredded there was little left of it, was exhibited to the rest of the army.

Most of the soldiers at Cambridge were from regions where the Indians had been gone for decades. They did not need rifles in order to survive, as did frontiersmen, so their guns were mostly the smoothbore musket. What they saw of the Pennsylvanians' marksmanship helped the other troops put up with the exasperating and unmilitary behavior of these riflemen.

Timothy Murphy and his comrades soon helped the American army tighten up on the British lines. When some Redcoat on guard duty patrolled his post at what he thought was a distance well beyond the range of any American gun and a bullet caught him in the leg, it resulted in a general withdrawal of British lines all the way around the town. The

British realized that with the arrival of these marksmen with their long guns a new element had been introduced into this war. Few of the King's army, including the officers, had ever even heard of a weapon with such long range. Duty on the lines now became much more arduous and dangerous.

Probably the masterpiece of the Riflemen at the siege of Boston was the work they did on the harbor side of the town. Here the British were accustomed to moving supplies by small boats well beyond the range of American muskets. But this was not beyond the range of the rifles, even though it was five hundred yards. From a low hill Timothy Murphy and his comrades laid a hail of bullets on a scow laden with provisions; the craft was riddled with holes and commenced to sink, while the men aboard all sustained hits. From then on British movement by boat was restricted.

The siege of Boston ended without a general battle, so the Riflemen did not have any heavy action. On March 17, 1776, when the artillery brought by Colonel Knox from Ticonderoga was emplaced at Dorchester Heights so as to command the main channel of Boston harbor, General Howe agreed to evacuate the town without a fight. After the British had sailed away forever, the American army marched to New York to prepare for an expected British attack there.

A year and a half were to pass before Timothy Murphy's big day arrived. We know he faithfully kept at soldiering, but nothing for the records of history occurred except that one night on a raid during some of the fighting in New Jersey, Tim and three comrades managed to capture the coach of a British general. This equipage they drove into the American lines with considerable uproarious hullabaloo.

Then, in the middle of 1777, the British evolved a plan

to strike a deadly blow at the cause of the American colonists. The plan was simple; it was to cut the colonies in two by a drive down from Canada, along Lake Champlain to the Hudson River, to meet another push up from New York City. New England, a hotbed of sedition, thus would be separated from the other nine colonies. Each of the separated regions then could be dealt with at leisure.

Burgoyne's powerful army began its march from Canada, and the Americans could do no more than snipe at them and obstruct roads. Except for an unfortunate and costly attempt to raid Bennington, Vermont, the British thrust southward was successful. It overran Fort Ticonderoga and Crown Point, swept light American forces aside and by the autumn was in country not far north of Albany. There Burgoyne encountered an army made up of every unit General Washington could find to defend the vital Hudson River valley. Included were Daniel Morgan's Rifles, an outfit of Virginian, Maryland and Pennsylvania marksmen, every man armed with the long gun that could so conclusively out-shoot any smooth-bore the British or the other colonial troops possessed.

For three weeks Burgoyne's army and the Americans hacked away at each other in forest and farm and in clearings, each side knowing that somewhere in this area the real battle would take place. Timothy Murphy was in Morgan's regiment, and with this sort of fighting in forest land and fields he was in his element. He and his comrade, David Elerson, firing from ambush, cut off British foraging parties, shot up the guard and brought in prisoners. On one occasion when Tim was skulking through the woods, Indian fashion, he heard a British sentry give the password. By using it himself, he contrived to get as far as the tent of a British officer.

He sauntered in and presented the point of his knife at the
abdomen of the astounded Englishman.

"Come with me or I let daylight into you," growled
Murphy.

The Redcoat, who saw that Tim possessed the present capability of doing exactly that, obeyed, and before long the two
of them came walking into the American lines.

On October 7, 1777, a decisive conflict occurred when a
strong force from Burgoyne's army advanced and ran into
heavy American fire at Freeman's Farm. Here Morgan's men
were a vital factor with their accurate long-range rifle fire,
and the British fell back, defeated at this point. Active in
this engagement was Benedict Arnold, who led one of the
American attacks.

It appeared the British might recover from this setback
when General Fraser, the most able officer in Burgoyne's
army, showed up with reinforcements. Quickly he turned
to reorganizing the defeated troops. He was everywhere, en-
couraging the men, stopping their retreat, turning them
about and putting fight into them. The drums began to roll;
the British counterattack, a bayonet charge, was ready to
commence. Every man who had ever faced a bayonet charge
of the Redcoats wished never to see another.

Daniel Morgan shouted out the names of a dozen of his
best marksmen.

"Men, that gallant officer is General Fraser," he told them.
"I admire him. I honor him. But it is necessary that he should
die. Victory for the enemy depends upon him. Do your duty."

They aimed and fired, all except Timothy Murphy, who
was busy climbing a small tree. He found a branch to use as
a gun rest and carefully sighted at General Fraser, who still

sat his horse three hundred yards distant in spite of the shots of the riflemen. When he was sure he had sighted dead on his target, he squeezed the trigger. The rifle spat fire and smoke, and the red-coated general rolled off his horse. Murphy still had his second barrel; again he squeezed the trigger and down went General Fraser's aide-de-camp.

With their leader gone, the British hesitated, and in this interval General Ten Broeck came up with three thousand New York troops, and the American advance was resumed. Not until the British were penned up in field fortifications they had constructed did the Americans stop. Burgoyne now was surrounded and beaten. He realized he could not win, and he had an idea that he could not successfully retreat to Canada with this large, aggressive army on his heels and the northern forests full of guerrillas to snipe at him and cut off his foraging parties. So Burgoyne decided to surrender.

This battle, known forever as Saratoga, is described by Creasy in his great work, *The Fifteen Decisive Battles*. It was decisive because it defeated a blow that could have been mortal to the American cause by splitting the colonies in two. And it was decisive because it made the French government realize the power of the American fighting men to the extent that France was now willing to make an alliance to help the colonists in their struggle for independence. This resulted in the aid of French money and supplies, a French fleet and, at last, a French army on American soil.

The turning point in the battle of Saratoga was Timothy Murphy and his rifle, the marksman who could fire a bullet that drove a nail into a tree. At three hundred yards he shot General Fraser out of his saddle and reversed the tide of the conflict. At the battlefield of Saratoga today there is a marker at the spot where Tim climbed the tree and took his careful aim.

After Saratoga, Timothy Murphy left Morgan's regiment to go to the aid of the settlers west of Albany. They were the victims of horrible outrages at the hands of Indian and Tory bands of scalping, murdering, burning raiders. Indeed, it appeared as if the farms of the Mohawk and Scoharie valleys might become wilderness again, the way the settlers were being killed and the buildings burned.

Help, however, was being sent to these frontiersmen, and Timothy Murphy was part of the group detached to go into the sort of country he knew so well. He spent the rest of the war there, gliding through the woods, scouting, rescuing captives, joining in the defense of settlements, always beating the Indians at their own game until at last he, and others, had made the lands beyond Albany safe to live in once more.

He was very good at what he was doing and very thorough. He told one person that he had scalped forty Indians, and to prove his statement he produced twenty of the scalps then and there. The surprising thing is that after this wild life he was able to settle down to the pursuits of peace, but that he did. He got married, had a farm and children and lived until 1818, a man with plenty of stories if anyone could get him to tell them.

8 ～～

Pepper Jack

WHEN COLUMBUS set sail into the unknown reaches of the Western Ocean, he was seeking a more direct route to the riches of the Orient. Since the time of the Roman Empire the spices of India and the islands, the tea of China, the rugs of Persia, the finely worked porcelain and brass objects from the lands of Eastern artisans, had come to Mediterranean shores by long and difficult land routes. By camel caravan across deserts and through mountain regions where bandit raids were always to be expected, the small and valuable loads made their way to the markets of Europe. The losses were high, and the quantity of merchandise was limited by the capacity of long lines of animals in the caravan. This tortuous method of transportation Columbus hoped to replace by the vastly more economical means of ships. If the world was round, India lay to the west, he reasoned, and there he hoped to arrive and open up a new route by which Oriental products would be carried to Europe.

One of the commodities most craved by the people of Europe was the pepper of India. This item, easily obtainable today at any grocery store or supermarket and found on every

housewife's shelf, was a rare commodity when the known
world was small. Pepper can do all sorts of things for anyone's cookery. It gave very common food an interesting taste,
then as today.

But pepper's usefulness extended far beyond what it did
for man's jaded taste. Pepper was one of the best preservatives
in a day before the mechanical refrigerator had even been
thought of. In New England blocks of ice harvested from
ponds in the dead of winter and carefully stored for use
throughout the year helped preserve food. This method was
not available in countries where the climate was too warm to
freeze a pond in winter, and this included the whole of the
Mediterranean area.

Pepper was the basic element in numerous recipes for preserving meat. One old favorite was half pepper and half
ginger. This was rubbed into the meat by someone who had
plenty of time and energy, and then the meat was hung in a
cool, dry place until it was time to use it. Until the twentieth
century, methods of preserving meat were of an importance
no one in this age of efficient mechanical refrigeration and
deep-freeze units can understand. Along with smoking meat
and pickling it in a salt solution, the pepper formulas were
of prime importance.

Columbus, thwarted by the huge barrier of the then unknown American continents, did not find the hoped-for easy
route to the Indies. Yet during the age of exploration, in
which he was so brilliant a figure, a route was found; indeed,
two routes: the passage around the Cape of Good Hope, which
generally is easy sailing, and the passage around Cape Horn,
which generally is not. Ships from the Western World at
last reached the Indies. Water-borne commerce flourished;

fortunes were made, and Europeans and Americans established trading posts, forts and spheres of influence in dozens of places in the Orient.

Yet after nearly three centuries of trade with the Indies the much sought after pepper was hardly more plentiful than in the time when it came over the difficult and dangerous caravan routes. The technique of getting pepper remained about the same; natives with baskets in the jungle searched for berries on plants growing wild much like the blueberry picker in a New England pasture or brush patch.

Then in 1788 and the years following occurred a combination of circumstances of great importance to Salem and other parts of the Yankee coast. The British were, of course, very active in the Orient. In Sumatra a few Englishmen in the employ of the East India Company went off on a venture of their own, the cultivation of pepper here and there in places in the jungles where the land was dry enough for a small plantation. It is most unlike the British to fail to seek out a market for any merchandise they have available, yet this was the fact. Successful they were in persuading Libbe Duppoh, one of the rajahs of northern Sumatra, to put his men to work cultivating pepper, yet they had no arrangements for shipping out the berries once they were harvested.

These Englishmen, called the Natal Concern, eventually saw an end to their marketing problem in the farsightedness of a Salem sea captain named Jonathan Carnes. In 1788, master of the *Cadet,* he traded along this coast and again in 1792, when he commanded the *Grand Sachem.* Since earliest times Sumatra, an island one thousand miles long, had been the source of small lots of pepper picked by the natives from bushes growing wild. Now he learned of the recently commenced project of the Natal Concern from whose plantations in obscure places in this equatorial land very considerable quantities of pepper could soon be expected.

Jonathan Carnes knew his Salem, a town where dwelt daring men who feared not to venture their ships and their capital in enterprises in any part of the world, no matter how remote or how dangerous. So he put his proposition up to the Peeles, who had the wherewithal to finance a voyage, and they gave him the schooner *Rajah*.

Heading south, this Salem vessel sailed down the Atlantic Ocean, rounded the Cape of Good Hope at the tip of Africa, then made the long reach across the Indian Ocean to the coasts of Sumatra, a half a world away from her home port. This voyage, in 1795, was uneventful, but the *Rajah*'s stay in Sumatran waters was not. Mindful that constant vigilance is the price of survival in this land of pirates and unpredictable natives, Captain Carnes saw to it that the watch was at all times alert, and his care was rewarded one dark night.

The vessel lay at anchor offshore after a day of trading for pepper. The bow watch, peering into the inky blackness of the tropic night, heard a suspicious noise from the water below the bowsprit and he let out a wild yell. On the quarterdeck Captain Carnes bellowed "All hands," seized a loaded musket from the rack and rushed forward, followed by his crew. They reached the forecastle just as heads appeared above the bulwark. The ship's cook straight-armed one of the boarders in the face and he disappeared, but another swung a cutlass and flicked off the cook's hand.

The *Rajah*'s men fired their muskets, and the heads disappeared. There were splashes, then silence as the Americans peered over the bulwarks into the darkness. They saw nothing. Then a voice floated over the water, speaking English but with a heavy French accent.

"Are you an American ship?"

"Schooner *Rajah* of Salem," shouted Carnes.

"We thought you were British until we heard zee voices of your men," came the voice. "We are a French privateer. We present out apologies and request permission to come alongside."

"Permission granted," bellowed Captain Carnes.

Battle lanterns cast a glow over the *Rajah*'s lee bulwarks as the French longboat drew up to the schooner's side.

"A big mistake," explained the man in the stern sheets. "We had not thought to see an American ship here. And now our lieutenant lies dead."

Indeed the lieutenant was dead. They saw his body lying in the bottom of the longboat, victim of one of the American musket balls. Carnes, glad to have this episode thus ended, nevertheless was not in the best humor.

"I see he is dead. And our cook has lost his right hand. Now get out of here before I give the rest of you a volley. And look out for American ships in the future."

"We will," said the Frenchman. Slowly the longboat rowed off into the darkness, and the *Rajah*'s watch on deck resumed their night patrol, while the watch below tumbled into their bunks. Captain Carnes, who, like every shipmaster, was also the ship's doctor, busied himself with stopping the bleeding from the raw stump where the enemy cutlass had sheered off the cook's hand.

The *Rajah* had no more bloody adventures on the Pepper Coast. Yet as the peppercorns were stowed in the vessel's hold until Carnes saw he was approaching the time when he would have a full cargo, he thought more and more of the hazard of this bold move taken by him and his owners.

"First time this has ever been done," he said to the mate. "What do you mean, sir?"

"First full cargo of pepper ever to be shipped into an American port," continued Carnes. "Our ships have picked up a few bags on voyages to these waters, but never a full cargo. No one ever was able to get that much pepper until these Britishers persuaded the natives to cultivate the pepper tree."

"Well, that's fine, isn't it?" queried the mate. "Makes it easy for us. What are you worrying about, Captain?"

"Lunkhead," snapped Carnes. "Did you ever think what a whole cargo of this stuff might do to the price of pepper in America?"

He turned and strode to his cabin. Indeed, why should the mate think of such things, he reflected. His task is to keep the crew busy making and taking in sail. It is up to the captain, and supercargo, if there is one aboard, to see to trading the rum, gin, tobacco and specie brought from the home port for some sort of cargo that will sell at a profit. Would this much pepper break the market? It was harder to figure than how to drive off a boatload or two of rapscallions who thought to seize the *Rajah*.

Finally loaded at Susu on Sumatra's northwest coast, the *Rajah* departed, leaving behind her a native ruler very much pleased with what he had made from these strange mariners from far beyond the seas.

Long weeks passed, and the schooner was again off the American coast, with Carnes still pondering in that loneliness that only a sea captain knows as to the wisdom of the next

step. Except for his owners, the Peeles, no one knew where
he had gone. The clearance papers filed at Salem when the
Rajah departed said she was bound for India, which in those
days meant anywhere in the vast uncharted waters of the
Orient.

Captain Carnes had not discussed navigation with the mate
once the vessel was in the East Indies. From remarks over-
heard, it appeared the crew thought this land of pepper was
part of India or perhaps Ceylon. To the mate he gave a strict
order to say nothing to identify in any way the place where
they had traded.

Then, a day's sail from Cape Cod, Captain Carnes made
his decision, laying a course not for Salem but for New York.
Unknown there, he nonetheless made a terrific commotion in
the shipping world when he arrived with a full cargo of
pepper. Merchants hurried to the wharf where the *Rajah*
lay, and Carnes heard them discussing their plans for putting
pepper aboard their ships bound for Havana, Port-au-Prince,
Naples, Málaga, Marseilles, Hamburg and Copenhagen.

There was not too much pepper; the price did not break.
Parceled out among the merchants of New York, it provided
dozens of small lots to be profitably traded in the ports of
Europe, the West Indies and South America. And for Captain
Jonathan Carnes, as he sat over his books of account, by the
light of the cabin's whale-oil lamp, there figured to be a
profit from this voyage of 700 per cent.

With a light heart he gave the order to cast off and make
sail for his home port, Salem. But if he had thought that
by going to New York his doings would be unknown, he was
much mistaken. When at last the *Rajah* was at her mooring
and the crew paid off, he learned that the news of his trans-

actions in New York had traveled ahead of him. Up and down Derby Street everyone seemed to know about his full cargo of pepper, to whom he sold it and for how much, and the wiseacres even had a startlingly close estimate of the profit on this long voyage to the Indies.

One fact was lacking. Where had he acquired this magnificent cargo? They asked him, and he smiled. They asked the crew when the men were sober and they asked them after spending considerable sums getting them drunk, but they got only vague and even ridiculous answers—India, Ceylon, Burma. Getting the mate drunk, which they did, was no more rewarding, for Jonathan Carnes had given him a wealth of data, in frequent conversations, that was wholly unsuitable for use by anyone planning a voyage. And the mate was of no mind to give up what secrets he did have, for he well knew upon which side his bread was buttered.

So the town of Salem, although it buzzed with talk of the exploit of their own Jonathan Carnes and his *Rajah,* had not one item of information valuable to any merchant or mariner hoping to get a cargo of pepper. This secret, remarkable when it is remembered how long these men had cruised the Sumatran coast or had been at anchor off Susu, continued to be kept until a day, a year later, when Carnes shipped another crew, entered "India" on the clearance papers and sailed off into the blue beyond Baker's Island.

The moment of his sailing was expected, for his preparations were known along the water front. Other vessels followed him, determined to discover the source of this fortune in pepper. Carnes well knew he would be followed. He was an excellent mariner and found it no trouble at all to lose the vessels whose skippers thought to find the easy way to the

Pepper Coast. A few changes of course in the blackness of night, and his pursuers discovered at dawn that they sailed in an ocean empty except for the dolphin and the albatross. And so Carnes again arrived off Susu with silver specie, interesting Yankee merchandise and plenty of rum to trade for the product of the secret pepper plantations.

When Carnes and his *Rajah* returned from the second Sumatra voyage, this time sailing directly to Salem, the cargo was an enormous 158,000 pounds of pepper. At the Custom House on Derby Street the owners paid a duty of $9,522, much to the delight of the Treasury Department, for the receipts from the port of Salem, at this point in the nation's history, accounted for one twentieth of all the revenues of the United States Government.

By this time the source of the pepper supply had ceased to be a secret. Following the first voyage, some of the more astute had guessed that Carnes had been to Sumatra, since earliest times known to be one of the few places on earth where pepper grows wild. Exactly where on this equatorial island, one thousand miles long, he had dropped anchor off the breakers of some coral reef had not been known until after his return from this second voyage.

How, then, was it revealed that Susu, Benkulen, Quallah Battu and Anabalu were the ports from which the pepper could be obtained? This time the crew were aware of the fact that the old port of Salem was pepper mad, and they knew the intense interest in the source of these little berries. They paid close attention to where they were and probably noted landmarks, penciled rough charts, took bearings and listened to any references to latitude and longitude. Whether the crew sold their knowledge for gold or let it slip while full of free drinks has never been determined, but whatever the way it became known, the knowledge of the Pepper Coast was all over town.

Now the door was open—wide. Nowhere in the world were there more daring shipowners or better mariners than in the Salem of that day. Nor were there anywhere men with a keener nose for a profit. So from this time on Jonathan Carnes, pioneer in the Sumatran pepper trade and discoverer of the Pepper Coast, was only one of the Salem shipmasters bringing into port the riches of the Indies. One after the other the big mercantile houses fitted out ships that departed for Sumatra. As the news spread, Boston ships and vessels from Philadelphia, New York, Providence and nearby Beverly set forth on this long voyage to the palm-fringed coast half a world away.

The result: the Americans took over the pepper trade of the world. From the ports of the Yankee coast it was shipped to all the countries of Europe, to the islands of the Caribbean, to South America, even to China. Fortunes were made, founded on the pepper trade, fortunes that built some of the most beautiful houses in North America today, the mansions of Chestnut Street, Salem, and Beacon Street, Boston, and the main streets of the smaller Yankee ports. And these fortunes, preserved by carefully drawn trusts and a tradition of respect for inherited principal, still exist and support the descendants of these early merchants to this day.

The Americans had excellent results in their trading with the Sumatrans, mainly for the reason that they treated the natives with more respect and friendliness than did the British and the Dutch. The Yankees were happy, although the British and the Dutch were not. They had both been much more active in Sumatra, yet the Americans, with their combination of daring industry and fair dealing with the natives, had walked away with the lucrative pepper business. England's famous East India Company, its finger in every pie in Asia, tried to get Britishers to stop selling any pepper in their possession to the Americans. This did not always work, for Yankee skippers rolled out kegs of Spanish silver dollars, as the British agents in this faraway island were usually athirst for hard money with which to carry on. And when a British agent did not wish to part with his pepper, the Yankee skipper went directly to the local potentates with excellent results.

An American skipper trading for pepper was obliged to anchor his vessel beyond the coral reefs and go ashore through the surf in the ship's boats. He had with him scales to weigh the pepper, and when he reached shore these scales were tested by the local rajah or *dato*. When both sides accepted them as accurate and the price per picul (133⅓ pounds) was agreed on, the ship fired three guns to signify that the contract was signed, sealed and delivered. Then the pepper was brought forth, weighed and stowed in the boats, and the Americans set forth on their perilous trip through the surf to their ship. At sundown, when trading ceased, the scales were locked in a big box ashore, and both sides posted a guard so there would be no tampering with the mechanism before business was resumed next day.

Considering the enormous amount of pepper purchased on this coast, there was very little trouble. That does not mean that the trade was harmonious at all times or that this was not a hazardous occupation. Boats turned over in the surf on the coral reefs, sometimes drowning a sailor. The dread tropical diseases, chiefly cholera and malaria, took their toll. The long wavy-bladed Malay dagger, the creese, accounted for many a Yankee mariner, perhaps in a robbery after dark or in a bamboo thicket where he had persuaded the woman of a Sumatran villager to go with him. The bones of many a young man from Essex County lie somewhere along the shores of the Pepper Coast.

Only occasionally was there cheating. An American skipper might succeed in doctoring the weights of the scales so that a picul came to more than 133⅓ pounds. The Sumatrans sometimes contrived to include clay and sticks and stones in the bags of pepper if they thought they were dealing with a captain who was easy to deceive. Piracy was rare, particularly in the early days. The natives of that coast were easy to get along with, but on the southeast shore of the island lived a Malay population to whom thievery and piracy seemed a normal life. The depradations of these rapscallions have colored the whole picture of the long years of the Sumatran trade.

No American shipowner in those days would have thought of sending a vessel to sea unarmed. Pistols, muskets, cutlasses and pikes were on hand for everyone, together with boarding nets to keep the enemy from coming over the bulwarks and cannon to give round shot and grape to any hostile craft. Usually a Malay proa, long and low, with a large crew and many oarsmen, could be taught manners with a broadside of four- and six-pound shot or a few whiffs of grape. The important point was to see to it they did not get close enough to board, for no American ship carried enough men to resist an attack by a hundred assailants.

In a few instances the pirates managed to get the better of the Americans in spite of all precautions. In 1805 the

Salem ship *Putnam* was lost because too many Malays were allowed on board at once. They produced their creeses, and the fight commenced. The Salem men, although losing several of their number, drove off the Malays with a struggle in which the heroic ship's carpenter, William Brown, used as his weapon a two-by-four timber four feet long, to which the cook had bolted his coffee grinder. Savagely swinging this dreadful instrument, he led those of his shipmates still unwounded, until the pirates were driven overboard, leaving one dead.

Captain Carlton was visiting one of two British ships at some distance when all this occurred, so the first mate was in command. This fellow, who had fled to the bowsprit when the attack commenced, now returned to the deck, still terrified, and insisted the crew take the longboat and row to the British ship for safety. This they did, whereupon the Malays returned, took possession of the *Putnam* and sailed her away. The ship was gone, and three of her crew were dead; certainly not a heroic story to be entered in the annals of the Yankee mariners.

The British ships sailed in pursuit in an effort to recapture the *Putnam*. They overtook her and the pirate craft, but when cannon balls began to fly, one of the British captains, as weak as the nameless first mate of the American ship, ordered his vessel to sheer off. This episode is unusual. If the behavior of Yankee seamen had ordinarily been as stupid as this, our ships could never have succeeded on the Pepper Coast or anywhere else. And certainly few Britishers ever were scared off by cannon balls or anything else.

Not until 1831 did pirates again get the best of an American vessel—really a remarkably good record. There had been numerous attacks in this period, all of them bloodily repulsed. This time the victim was the ship *Friendship* at Quallah Battu, and again it was lack of vigilance while the captain was ashore that permitted Malays who came aboard to trade to turn upon the crew and take the ship. Captain Endicott and four men ashore buying pepper saw clearly what had happened, so they made a quick escape from Quallah Battu and rowed twenty-five miles up the coast to the port of Muckie, where lay three American ships. With them in their escape by boat was Po Adam, that well-known friend of Yankee mariners, a small rajah who had a fort at Pulo Kio, three miles south of Quallah Battu.

Taking a grave view of this piracy, the three American captains at Muckie immediately prepared to sail to Quallah Battu to recapture Captain Endicott's *Friendship*. These ships, the *James Monroe, Palmer,* and *Governor Endicott,* made a strong squadron to deal with the pirates, who now had the *Friendship* close inshore under the guns of the Quallah Battu forts.

American merchantmen of that day were well armed, and the forts scared them not at all. Indeed, they opened a bombardment that silenced the hostile guns. Then they mounted a small boat attack on the captured *Friendship,* but no blood was shed, for the Malays took to their boats and fled. When the Americans boarded their ship, they found every movable object had been stolen: clothes, dishes, nautical instruments, specie, blankets, muskets, powder and cutlasses, rope and sails, needles, charts—everything except cannon and the barrels of salt beef.

With the help of Po Adam of Pulo Kio, the nautical instruments were bought back from these thieves, but nothing else.

As for the clothes, they adorned the natives, and one Sumatran strutted about in the town wrapped in the red tablecloth from the captain's cabin. With the repurchased nautical instruments and equipment from the other American vessels, the *Friendship* was able to sail for home. Four of the sailors had escaped, finally finding refuge in Po Adam's fort. Four more who were wounded had been sheltered by Chinese merchants. So these and the men who were with Captain Endicott were enough to work ship on the homeward-bound passage.

Because of other attempts on ships, Quallah Battu had a bad reputation in the Western World. Upon the arrival of the *Friendship* at Salem, her owners, smarting under the losses this attack had caused them, at once sent a vigorous protest to the President, who referred it to the Navy Department. The frigate *Potomac,* already under orders to sail to China, was instructed to go to Quallah Battu for what might be termed a visit of instruction. Detachments of sailors and marines from the frigate's complement of five hundred were landed by night to attack the town's five forts. Four of the forts were captured, dismantled and burned.

The fifth fort, more stubborn than the rest, required a bombardment by the *Potomac*'s thirty-two-pounders. This attack completely destroyed it. Peace followed, with gifts of coconuts, fruit and sugar cane. The leaders were brought aboard the frigate to view the long rows of thirty-two-pounders on the gun deck, and they promised to leave Americans alone in the future.

This lesson was forgotten by the Sumatrans, for in 1837 an attack was made on the *Eclipse* at Muckie which resulted in the murder of the captain and one of the crew as well as the theft of every movable object on board. This time the U.S. Navy sent two vessels, the *Columbia* and *John Adams*. No redress could be obtained from the rajah of Muckie, so the forts were destroyed by the guns of the ships, and the town and all boats were burned by a landing party.

The glorious days of the pepper trade began to fade. By 1846, when the last pepper cargo entered Salem, one hundred and seventy-nine shiploads had been brought into this famous port. Other American vessels carried on in a limited way until shortly after 1870, but new influences were at work that changed the nature of this trade.

The Civil War dealt a blow to American shipping from which it was slow to recover. Foreigners got much of the trade with steamships that were very much faster than the best of the American clippers. This was a time when the development of our Western territories claimed our capital and adventurous young men of the sort that had given us leadership at sea.

Another influence was a new system of trade developed by the brilliant Englishman, Sir Stamford Raffles, the man who founded and developed the city of Singapore. This system was the free trade entrepôt, a point to which all merchandise was brought by producers, no matter how large or small the quantity. When the genius of Raffles had succeeded in getting this system working, the pepper of Sumatra was taken in small Malay ships to Penang or Singapore, from whence it was loaded aboard larger British ships.

Once Salem was the pepper capital of the world, much to the distress of the English. Yet over the years they patiently developed their system of attracting merchandise to their great shipping points. So finally British ships carried the pepper, and London became the pepper capital of the world.

For Salem and other ports remained the memories of the trade, the romantic names of faraway Oriental ports, the fine mansions built with the profits and the fortunes that were made when this area was the world's pepper pot.

One old merchant of Salem, so it is said, was obsessed in his later days with the fear that he might be put in the tomb before he was dead. Apparently what he thought was that his physician and family might think something in the nature of a coma was actually death and that later he might awake in his coffin with the lid screwed tightly on.

To eliminate this possibility he exacted from his wife and his three sons the solemn promise that his coffin would remain in his house and not be closed and conveyed to the graveyard until thirty days after he had been pronounced dead. When his time came it was July, and the execution of the promise presented certain practical problems.

His ingenious family, to prevent the old gentleman from decaying in weather when the glass was ninety every day, went to the warehouse, obtained three piculs of pepper and packed the inside of the coffin completely, so only the face of their revered sire was visible. This was completely effective. The thirty days passed, and the presence of his unburied body in the drawing room in no way discommoded anyone.

On the thirty-first day he was conveyed to the cemetery, and his coffin, the lid now on, was placed in the family vault. This was in 1831, and there his mortal frame remained until a day in 1948, when a couple of his great-great-grandsons went up to the cemetery with some workmen to see about repairing the iron door of the tomb.

While they had the door off, they examined the coffins and

found the lid of this one loose, so they lifted it out of morbid curiosity. But what they saw inside troubled them not at all. There lay their ancestor in his eternal bed of pepper, perfectly preserved and looking exactly like the portrait of him that hung in the long drawing room of the family mansion on Chestnut Street, Salem. Everyone present had a look, and they regretted that no camera had been brought along. Then they nailed the cover of the coffin, confident that if the nails rusted away or the oak rotted in the next one hundred and seventeen years, he would be here in his pepper berries, in good condition to greet whoever might have the task of attending to repairs.

9

Big Sixes and Long Nines

ON THIS BRIGHT July day in 1799 the last cartload of sugar had
rumbled down Derby Wharf, to be slung aboard and stowed
below. The last man to join the crew had come over the side,
sea chest on his shoulder, making his way to the forecastle to
find himself a bunk. Men on the wharf loosened the hawsers
made fast to the bollards; the longboat rowed out into the
harbor with a towline, and the fore-topsail and headsails were
shaken from their harbor furls to catch the gentle westerly
breeze.

As the ship inched away from the pier, green harbor water
showed wider between her sides and the pilings of the wharf.
The sails tightened and bellied out as they caught the light
westerly airs. As she made out into the stream and the crew
got more sail onto her, a well-dressed man standing apart from
the crowd on the wharf watched every move. He seemed
satisfied as the vessel moved down Salem harbor toward Fort
Pickering, pleased with the sight of this ship, her tall masts,
her fast lines, the smart way the crew handled her. Occasionally the little smile on his lips vanished and lines of pain
momentarily crossed his face.

Alone he stood on the crowded wharf, for in Salem it was understood that a shipowner is not to be disturbed on the day his vessel departs. He is to be left alone with his thoughts as ship and cargo gradually grow smaller in the distance of the bay, bearing a sizable part of his fortune on a voyage of a year or more, which is exposed every hour of every day of that time to the perils of the sea and the hazards of trading in ports a half a world away. And exposed, in this year 1799, to the attacks of French privateers, prowling the seas in search of American merchantmen.

Left alone to watch his departing vessel was this merchant of Salem, Elias Hasket Derby, owner of fourteen ships. King Derby he was called, because he stood first in this town; first in wealth and in ships owned, first to send a vessel to many a port where the American flag had never before been seen, first in new ideas to extend Yankee commerce and increase the prosperity of Salem town. One man only felt privileged to invade King Derby's privacy at this moment. The Reverend William Bentley, minister of Salem's East Church, when any of the town's activities interested him, never hesitated to go where he pleased, talk to anyone and ask all sorts of questions. And this erudite clergyman was the one person in town whom no one ever resented.

"Hello, Reverend." Derby smiled. "I'm ready for your questions. But first let me tell you a little about my ship, the *Mount Vernon,* which in a very few minutes now will be taking her departure from Baker's Island. I planned her, every timber and sail and gun in her, for this strange war we are now fighting with the French."

"A strange war indeed, Mr. Derby," agreed the rotund Reverend Bentley. "And yet it makes some sense from their point of view. Number one, if the French capture ships going to or from an English port or the port of a British colony or ships with English goods aboard, they have hurt to a degree their mortal enemy, England. Number two, if they stretch a point and gobble up American ships that have no British goods aboard and never go near an English port, then the French treasury will wax fat at our expense. The French need money to fight England."

Derby's face darkened.

"My dear Bentley, I agree with every word you say. But mind you, I've planned it so the French rascals will not have a cent of my money."

"And your ship has cleared for Mediterranean ports?" Bentley seemed incredulous. "You are to trade right under the enemy's nose?"

"Precisely, Bentley," snapped King Derby. "See? My *Mount Vernon* is up with Baker's. But as I started to say, I have planned it so those confounded revolutionary rapscallions must work very hard before they lay hands on anything belonging to the house of Derby."

"How, sir?"

"This way. Did you notice the lines of the *Mount Vernon?* Fast. I worked with Retire Becket over here in his shipyard to make this the fastest merchantman afloat. Squint at my ship, Reverend, way out there now between Baker's Island and Gale's Point. A light breeze, so they are setting the studding sails. Can you see the ringtail, that sail on the slender mast aft of the mizzen? And she has water sails, the booms going out from the deck and the sail reaching downward. Those catch light airs. Of course, if the wind freshened and we got a bit of a sea, they would carry away before the crew

could get them in, so we put round holes in the lower edges
of our water sails, so the waves, or part of them, will go right
through. No, sir, no privateer can catch my ship, even if it is
nearly a flat calm."

"And if the enemy should catch up?"

King Derby laughed.

"I will only say I would like to be there."

Far to the east of Baker's now, the ship was fading from
sight.

The Reverend Bentley seemed puzzled. Derby, obviously
pleased with himself, continued.

"She carries twenty six-pounders. No measly four-pounders
for me. They'll do for Malay pirates but not for French privateers. And when the Frenchman wears ship and gets astern
so he can fire a raking broadside that will go tearing down
the length of my ship, giving him a chance of hits on mizzen
and main and foremasts and sails and rigging and also the
men at the guns, well, I have a surprise for him."

"Surprise?"

"Yes, Reverend. No cabins for the officers of the *Mount
Vernon*. Let them sleep on the deck. The cabin has two nine-
pounders firing through the stern ports. Nine-pounders, man.
And fifty in the crew. If two French vessels turn up, we can
man both broadsides."

"Mr. Derby, I see now why you would like to be there. I
am a man of the cloth, yet I, too, must admit I would like to
be there."

The two men turned to walk together up the wharf, past
other ships moored alongside and barrels and boxes and crates
stacked in front of the warehouses. The *Mount Vernon* was
gone. Beyond the horizon she was bowling along with fair

winds and a quartering breeze, now beyond the sight of the man who had planned her.

"Mr. Derby, your vessel is now in the hands of Providence," said Bentley.

"Yes. And in the hands of a stout Salem crew and her captain. My son is in command, Reverend." The merchant spoke proudly. "Captain Elias Hasket Derby, Junior."

East of the Azores came the first big test for the *Mount Vernon*. Dead ahead the masthead lookout saw an enormous fleet of men-of-war sailing in a half-moon formation, fifty vessels in all, reaching for miles. Here young Captain Derby faced decision. If he turned and ran, he would arouse suspicion, and then would commence a long stern chase. This fleet he thought to be British, and their policy had always been to chase a suspicious vessel for days, if need be. So he sailed straight ahead, a course leading him right through the center of this great armada.

Then he discovered this was not part of the British fleet. It was a concentration of the French navy and its allies, the Spaniards. And France was the enemy. Too late now to change course; he sailed on.

Signal pennants fluttered from the halyards of the French flagship. Then from each far wing of the fleet a swift frigate turned to pursue the Yankee ship, while from the center, much nearer, a sloop of war came about to join in the chase. Here was the first test for the ship that was the pride of the house of Derby. And as for the first phase of the test, she responded superbly with her speed, easily outsailing the frigates.

The sloop of war, near at hand, was not to be eluded. The unsuspecting Derby had no idea that cannon balls would soon be flying, and when the French vessel gave him a broadside, he was taken completely by surprise. Why he was so innocent as to let himself be taken by surprise is not at all clear. He knew every French vessel was an enemy; he was within gunshot, and yet this broadside caught him wholly unprepared.

However, the young captain's innocence vanished forever in the roar of this ferocious broadside. Orders cracked out aboard the *Mount Vernon;* crews raced to the great guns, breechings were unloosed, powder monkeys ran to the magazines, and the ship quickly cleared for action. Then the windows in the American's stern were triced up, the nine-pounders roared, and the heavy cannon balls crashed through the French rigging, smashing yards, clipping braces and halyards.

Derby swung his ship, gave the enemy a broadside of six-pound balls and then came about to give the crews of the nine-pounders, now reloaded, another chance. Aboard the French man-of-war splinters flew, and one of the ship's boats was stove in. Holes opened in the sails, and the fractured fore-topsail yard drooped. The French had all they wanted of Yankee gunfire. The sloop of war sheered off in a wide circle and did not renew the chase until he was a mile and a half astern.

There the French man-of-war was in an excellent position, for his fleet was now so far distant that the admiral would think he was in hot pursuit. Yet he was also far enough from the deadly gunfire of this American merchantman so that he was safe, with time to repair his damaged rigging and send his wounded sailors to the surgeon. Darkness fell and the chase continued. The Frenchman from time to time fired a signal rocket to inform his commander he still was carrying out orders by pursuing the American. When the sun rose, the French vessel was gone, returned to his fleet to report that his ship had not caught this strange merchantman with the lethal sting in its tail.

This was only a beginning. Before the *Mount Vernon* reached Gibraltar, she was engaged in numerous brushes with enemy privateers, each time either outsailing them or letting them have enough round shot to convince them that this was not the day to get rich at the expense of the Americans.

The biggest ordeal came in the Straits of Gibraltar, when a large privateer swarming with a crew of one hundred men tackled the *Mount Vernon*. This time there was no surprise, no hesitation. The Salem men were veterans by now, used to battle and confident of what their guns could do. Immediately they went to work on their enemy.

A broadside of grapeshot turned the privateer's decks into a shambles. Another broadside of bar shot cut and tore at his sails. Then Derby bore away, fired his nine-pounder stern guns and veered for another broadside. This flogging was too much for the privateer; he struck his flag and rolled helplessly in the trough of the sea.

Here was an opportunity for young Captain Derby to board the enemy and carry her into Gibraltar as a prize. But he did not do so. Judgment is the most important quality of all in any voyage, and here he needed the very best. What enemy vessel lurked beyond Algeciras Point? If he put part of his crew aboard the helpless enemy, might that be the moment when more French vessels would bear down on him as his *Mount Vernon* tried to shepherd this badly damaged craft into Gibraltar?

So he left her there, sailing into Gibraltar to receive the congratulations of the British naval officers, who had seen it all. "A satisfaction to flog the rascal in full view of the English fleet," he wrote in his letter to his father, when at last he was at anchor in the harbor with time to sit down, pen in hand.

As to guns, the captain wrote that two nine-pounders are better than eight six-pounders. He was in a position to know; he had both nines and sixes. He went on to say that two long twelves would do better than twenty six-pounders. Certainly any merchant captain would have been delighted with twelve-pounders, which was a gun used as part of a frigate's armament, yet there were not many merchant vessels of that day large enough to furnish a suitable firing platform for a twelve-pounder. The sloops of war of that era carried sixes and sometimes nines as their heaviest armament.

In the course of his letter Captain Derby wrote that an American warship should always be on patrol in this area. He said he could see as he wrote two American ships being captured by French privateers. The British Lord St. Vincent, in a fifty-gun ship bound for England, promptly retook one of the American ships, but the other was taken by the French into the Spanish port of Algeciras. There the ship and cargo would be condemned as a prize and the crew robbed and tossed into prison or left penniless to beg.

Captain Derby was not long in Gibraltar. He had sugar to sell and he heard the price was good in Italy, so he went about his business. With him sailed another American ship, glad to have the protection of Derby's powerful guns. At Palermo the price of sugar did not suit him, so he sailed to Naples,

Colonel Leslie and his British regiment are thwarted by the raising of the bridge across the North River at Salem while Parson Barnard persuades the Colonel to keep the peace. Painting by Bridgman.

A Minuteman receives word that the British
are approaching and hastens to join others on
their way to battle.

Minutemen along the Lexington-to-Boston
road fire at the retreating British from behind
a stone wall.

An early drawing of the Battle of Bunker Hill
shows (left to right) the Boston battery, bombarding British warships, Charlestown in
flames, British troops attacking up the slopes
and American troops, erroneously portrayed in
the open when they actually were protected by
a fort.

General Howe, left foreground, directs the evacuation of British
troops from Boston, while men at the right push cannons into the
water to keep them from rebel hands.

The guns of **Ticonderoga** are hauled over rough terrain on the long
journey to General **Washington's** army besieging **Boston.**

The *Mount Vernon* of Salem, most famous armed merchant ship of the Derby fleet, defeats a French privateer off Gibraltar.

A typical coastal scene showing Crowninshield's Wharf, Salem, Massachusetts, about 1800, one of a half-dozen busy wharves with

vessels always arriving and departing. Painting by George Ropes, a famous marine artist of that era.

The burning of the frigate *Philadelphia* in Tripoli Harbor, showing the U.S.S. *Intrepid* (left) escaping after boarding the captured American man-of-war and setting her on fire.

The blowing up of the fire ship *Intrepid* in Tripoli Harbor.

The frigate *Constitution* is pursued into Marblehead harbor by two British frigates in the War of 1812. Painting by John Leavitt.

This sketch by Captain Porter shows the frigate *Essex* refitting at Nukahiva in the South Pacific island of Marquesas, surrounded by five captured British ships.

The American frigate *Essex* fighting the *Phoebe* and *Cherub* in Valparaiso harbor before her surrender to the two British men-of-war.

The Cunard steamship *Britannia* departs from Boston on schedule through a channel in the ice made by Yankee ice cutters from the many ponds in the region where ice was harvested.

"Old Floyd Ireson for his hard heart,
Tarred and feathered and carried in a cart
By the women of Marblehead."
Drawing of *Skipper Ireson's Ride* by Alfred Fredericks.

where he made a very profitable sale.

Then came the problem of a return cargo, for no merchant who sailed home with an empty ship could expect to prosper. The art was to sell cargo from America at a good figure, then look about for merchandise selling cheap that was likely to be in demand at home.

This Captain Derby did. He contracted for 700 casks of wine and $60,000 worth of ormuzine silk not yet manufactured. How to use the long wait until the silk was ready was a problem. He was entertained by Lord Nelson, Admiral of the British fleet, then at Naples, and by Lady Hamilton. The admiral and the captain had a fine time discussing naval tactics, while Nelson's lovely paramour listened—and probably yawned.

The practical Captain Derby doubtless found this famous and scandalous romance completely uninteresting. With his mind on making money for the house of Derby, opportunity soon came his way. Wheat was cheap at Manfredonia on the Adriatic or eastern coast of Italy; wheat was high at Leghorn on Italy's western coast, far up the peninsula, not a great distance from the French border.

Taking some of the money from the sale of the sugar, he purchased two polacca rigged ships, and with the *Mount Vernon* as escort, he sailed around the southern tip of Italy to Manfredonia to buy wheat. Again he ran into trouble, this time two marauding armed Turkish vessels whose commanders thought to make easy captures of this little fleet. The Turks immediately found themselves targets of a storm of cannon fire. One, with his side planking stove in, began to settle in the water. The other came alongside to help him, and the Americans sailed onward with their wheat.

By the time this merchandise was delivered to Leghorn and the ships had returned to Naples, the silk was ready to be stowed in the *Mount Vernon*'s hold. The wine casks were placed in the lower part, then some brass cannon Derby had purchased, and finally the long packages containing bolts of silk were put on the upper layer, riding above any danger of salt water always to be found in the bilge of a ship.

Selling the polaccas, which they had used to pick up a smart profit freighting the wheat from Manfredonia to Leghorn, they headed west for home, with the Derby brig *Cruger* in company. No French privateers appeared to annoy the two American vessels, although the gunners were prepared, and powder and ball lay ready at all times.

Young Captain Derby was a proud skipper when once again he sighted Baker's Island, from which point he had taken his departure more than a year earlier. As he stood on the quarter-deck while his vessel came down the main ship channel, close to Beverly's bold, rocky shores, he ran over in his mind all the things he had to tell his father and he wondered whether the cargo he had brought back could command a good price here in America. Upon this one fact depended the success or failure of the voyage. Merchandise brought to a glutted market hardly paid the freight; on the other hand, the merchant whose vessel arrived with scarce commodities found a golden harvest.

The *Mount Vernon* found Salem receptive to her cargo. So well received were the choice Italian silks and the casks of wine in this country of rum and beer that the voyage netted, after all the expenses of ship and crew, the astounding profit of $100,000. All Salem buzzed with the stories of what the guns of the *Mount Vernon* had done not only to the French and Turkish privateers but to a vessel of the French navy itself.

In the grogshops and taverns along the water front mugs were raised and toasts were drunk whenever one of her crew appeared. Every detail of the operations of the long nine-pounders in the stern was listened to with closest attention. Salem's maritime population christened the ship "the little frigate" and engaged in happy estimates of what she would do to the French privateers the next time she put to sea.

But Captain Elias Hasket Derby, Junior, was not able to tell his father the details of their naval victories and their trading successes. His father was gone, at last the victim of the internal disorders that had plagued him so many years without being able to subdue his active mind and his magnificent capability for successful planning.

Elias Hasket Derby was sixty when he sailed to his last anchorage—not an old man, but one who might have expected many more years of mercantile activity. Yet in achievement his life was a long one. No man had done more to bring Salem to its position as one of the great ports of America, perhaps of the world.

His vessels had sailed to places where no American ship had traded before. He had made a fortune and he had given employment to hundreds. At the last he had designed and built a ship which, because of the expert planning that went into her, was one of the very first to show the world that a vessel flying the American flag is not to be trifled with by anyone.

10

Not One Cent for Tribute

PROBABLY NEVER in the long history of the United States Navy has there been a stranger mission than that of the U.S.S. *George Washington* in 1800. Before this man-of-war's cruise ended, there had been added to the ship's original mission various operations beyond the orders of the Navy Department that it would not have been thought possible for Americans to be called on to perform.

The *George Washington*'s orders were to proceed to Philadelphia and load the cargo that the United States Government was sending to Algiers on the Mediterranean coast of Africa as the annual tribute owed to that regency. There was occasion to use all speed with this mission, for messages from Richard O'Brien, American consul at Algiers, made it clear that the Dey, who ruled that land, was becoming increasingly angry with the tardiness of the United States Government in fulfilling its obligations to pay tribute under the treaty.

War, warned O'Brien, would soon be the result if the Dey of Algiers did not receive his payments of tribute more promptly. And war with Algiers could be a national disaster,

118

for American merchant ships in the Mediterranean were numerous. Should the Dey of Algiers declare war, his corsairs would sail forth to capture the Yankee vessels. Ships and cargoes would be sold, the proceeds poured into the already overflowing Algerian treasury and the sailors would become slaves until ransom money arrived to buy them out of their servitude. The price of ransom was three thousand dollars per sailor.

There was, in the American Government, no guesswork about this. The dealings with the four regencies of the Barbary Coast—Morocco, Algiers, Tunis and Tripoli—were prescribed exactly in a manner quite unusual in the world of diplomacy.

The reason that the results of failure to pay tribute could be accurately predicted was simple. Before the United States Government had concluded treaties with the Barbary Powers, their corsairs had seized American ships whenever and wherever they found them. Our vessels, and those of other weak nations, the Barbary chieftains considered to be mere trespassers on the face of the waters. Until such a nation as Denmark, Sweden, Naples, Ragusa or America got permission by treaty, payments of tribute and annual presents to sail those seas within range of the corsairs, their ships were liable to capture and confiscation, and their mariners became slaves in Barbary.

This was a system. Under it the weak nations lost many a ship and cargo, and at one time seven hundred Christians were slaves in Algiers alone. Some were ransomed; some died of hard labor; many were carried off by recurrent visitations of the plague. The United States Government came to terms with these Barbary pirate governments. It had to. By treaty it was agreed how much the Americans were to pay.

Strangely enough, the Barbary rulers preferred merchandise to money. These primitive potentates dearly loved to have expensive baubles made by the hands of European craftsmen, perhaps because in the Mohammedan world there was almost no artisan capable of making these things. In the official records of those days appear lists of objects bought by United States agents for our consul to give as presents to the Bashaw of Tripoli, the Bey of Tunis, the Dey of Algiers or the Emperor of Morocco. A list of such items is a valuable indication of what sort of men were the rulers of the Barbary Powers and what the United States Government was up against in trying to placate them.

Our consul at Tripoli purchased from the mercantile house of Joseph Cohen Bacri & Co. the following presents to give the Bashaw and Grandees of Tripoli:

    3 caftans of brocade
    1 gold watch "diamonded" and a chain
    2 gold repeating watches
   10 silver plain watches
    1 gold snuffbox
    2 gold chains
    8 silver gilt snuffboxes
    1 large diamond ring, solitaire
    2 small diamond rings, solitaire
    6 dozen handkerchiefs

The foregoing cost the United States Treasury $2930.

In 1797, at the conclusion of peace with Tunis, our government gave rings and watches and chains in about the same quantity. For Tunis there was also "one gold snuff box with musick," "one gold watch rich in diamonds" and "four snuff boxes—tortoise shell."

Richard O'Brien, United States consul at Algiers, in 1797 wrote that the Dey of Algiers demanded the following:

some "elegant" penknives
some small gilt thimbles
scissors cases
"Calculated for the Queen and daughter a few shawls with roses curiously wrought in them."
"A few rosed China Cups and twenty pounds of fine tea for the Prime Minister."
"A few fineries and a few Crates of Plates."

Upon another occasion the Navy Department purchased for the Dey of Algiers eight India shawls with figures and two pieces of finest India muslin sprigged with gold. The choicest gift of all was purchased in London for the Bey of Tunis. H. W. Mortimer, Gun Makers to His Majesty and the Honorable East India Company, at the order of the United States Government, made specially the following: one gun, gold barrel, stock decorated with helmets, battle axes, pikes, swords, drums, halberds, bows and arrows, flags, cannon, shields, fruit and flowers, with diamonds and emeralds appearing here and there on the weapon. For this extraordinary piece of ordnance the gun makers to His Majesty made a mahogany case lined with crimson velvet.

Item two was a pair of gold pistols with the same decoration of warlike objects upon the wooden butts, and doubtless the fruit and flowers, although they seem incongruous amid such a collection of lethal weapons.

The third item was five gold-mounted guns, and of these the gun maker's bill said "superior to any ever finished in this Kingdom." The superiority undoubtedly lay in decoration rather than in range or accuracy.

Then appear in the bill five pairs of gold-mounted pistols, the last entry in the list of weapons for the Bey of Tunis and his Court to use when dressed for state occasions.

It is set forth that the total of this bill paid by the United States Government for these golden shooting irons purchased to please the pirate ruler of Tunis came to 6809 pounds, which was about $33,000. It would be interesting to know how these guns performed when they were fired. Data on this point is wholly lacking, perhaps because these swaggering barbarians were content to use them merely for display. And it should be added that our government's expenditure to pamper His Highness may have been an excellent investment, for Tunis was the least troublesome of the four Barbary regencies.

Indeed, from the Bey of Tunis there came certain expressions of Mohammedan courtesy which seem to indicate he was more of a gentleman, or at least less of a rapscallion, than those who occupied the other thrones of Barbary. In one document of truce with the United States he referred to our President as "the selected chief among the community of Jesus, Washington, the present ruler of America."

Much is implicit in this brief statement. In it we may see the attempt of a North African semi-civilized despot to understand the nature of an election. The idea of a head of state who arrived at his eminence in any way except by inheritance or by the murder or ousting of the person who was occupying the position was very hard for him to grasp. He had heard of this curious procedure the Americans termed an election, and his phrase, "the selected chief," is a fairly good understanding of the process. Even better comprehension is shown when he speaks of the "present" ruler of America. One used to a country where a ruler never stopped ruling until he died of natural causes, was opened up with a scimitar, or was deposed and exiled would find it hard to realize that a president would cease to be in office if on Election Day the voters chose someone else. Yet he did understand this, for he wrote "present ruler."

Again, in the Tunisian treaty of 1800, the Bey referred to our President as "the most distinguished and honored President of the Congress of the United States of America, the most distinguished of those who profess the religion of the Messiah, of whom may the end be happy." Here he thinks of Congress as some sort of junta controlling the United States. The idea of a president of all the people, and elected by them, was too much for him. He was polite enough to wish the President a happy end, by which he doubtless meant a death from natural causes at the end of life's course instead of a sudden decease resulting from a bullet, a knife, poison in his wine or from being thrown from the battlements of the castle.

This Mohammedan, the Bey of Tunis, referred to the United States as "the community of Jesus" and the President as the "most distinguished of those who profess the religion of the Messiah." Maybe he so wrote to make it abundantly plain that the United States was not Mohammedan. Possibly it appeared to him that the United States was more Christian than other nations. He says so plainly. Other Christian nations, particularly Spain, would have been somewhat annoyed had they known such a view was held by the ruler of a nation as important as Tunis. Most likely, however, is that these ornate compliments were used whenever he wrote an

important missive to the head of another state and that
Napoleon or the Czar of Russia or the King of Spain would
be similarly complimented as the leader of the Christian
world.

Gold watches, gold coins, rings, snuffboxes, gold-mounted
pistols and guns, no matter how attractive to the rulers of
Barbary and their grandees, were not as precious as naval
stores, ship timbers, masts, cordage, gun carriages. The mu-
sical snuffbox was only a bauble, but live-oak ship timber
or North Carolina tar or great oars fashioned of ash by Yankee
craftsmen were the very lifeblood of these pirate regencies,
and American marine materials were the world's finest.

So we find the Dey of Algiers refusing $30,000 cash from
the United States Government in payment of its annual
tribute and demanding shipbuilding materials. At one time
the Dey extracted from the United States agents the promise
of a thirty-six-gun frigate as that year's price of peace. And
he got his frigate, the *Crescent,* built at Portsmouth, New
Hampshire, a fine ship turned over to the Dey to use as a
piratical corsair. The United States Government delivered
the *Crescent,* well knowing its probable destiny, because the
Dey had to be pleased.

It was an installment of tribute due Algiers that the U.S.S.
George Washington was ordered to transport in 1800. What
befell her on this voyage is one of the strangest pages in our
naval history.

This shipment was late. Indeed, the United States was a
couple of years in arrears, and every letter from Richard
O'Brien, the American consul in Algiers, contained accounts
of the exasperation of the Dey of Algiers and his threats to
let loose his corsairs on the Yankee merchantmen plying the

Mediterranean with valuable cargoes. So imminent was the danger of war that our government hurried. Instead of looking about for one of our merchant ships to carry the cargo of tribute, the frigate *George Washington* was ordered to Philadelphia to load. Some of her guns were removed to make room for cargo and her crew was reduced.

The ship, however, still had fifteen guns which she well needed, for in 1800 we were engaged in a naval conflict since termed the "Quasi War with France." The French privateers were capturing American vessels wherever they found them. The cargo of tribute to Algiers would not have been safe in a merchantman, but the *George Washington,* even with her reduced armament, was quite capable of dealing with any privateer.

At Philadelphia she took aboard the various things that the Dey of Algiers had made known that he desired. An examination of the cargo list will serve not only to show what were the needs of this seafaring nation on the North African shore, but also what things American produced which were valued abroad. The list follows:

77 pieces of seasoned oak plank
 2 transoms (for the stern of a ship)
24 pieces of heavy keel timber
10 stern pieces
 2 stern posts (for the rudder)
117 pieces of 2½-inch white oak plank. (These were very heavy pieces for the side of a ship and not easy to obtain in a country of North Africa, where forests are few.)
51 pieces of floor lumber
143 three-inch planks
522 oars and sweeps. (The sweeps were enormous oars

used to row a large ship in a calm and were often
manned by "galley slaves.")

     8 masts
     1 bowsprit
   100 barrels of pitch
   100 barrels of tar
   100 barrels of turpentine
   100 barrels of rosin

(The foregoing four items were very useful in calking a
vessel to make it watertight and were produced from American pine forests in the South.)

One hundred and fifty barrels of gunpowder, 300 coils of
cordage and 100 pieces of canvas are items useful to the
Algerian navy, as were 3 cables and 8 gun carriages. A lot of
15 boxes of lampblack would be used in mixing paint. Two
lion heads, carved and painted to life, were included. These
were for decoration of the ends of the catheads, horizontal
timbers projecting from the sides of the ship near the bow.
The anchors, when raised, were made fast to the catheads.

In addition to these naval supplies, the cargo of tribute
contained a quantity of choice products not native to America
but common in our ports because American ships were trading in every part of the world and bringing home foreign
merchandise in quantity. So, as part of his tribute, the Dey
of Algiers received the following:

     1 box of fine loaf sugar (a West Indies product)
     1 tierce of green coffee (from the West Indies or possibly
        Arabia)
     8 bags of pepper (grown in Sumatra)
     4 boxes of china. (These dishes were brought from Can-
        ton in the bilge of a ship carrying tea. The bilge is
        likely to be wet and tea stowed there would be

NOT ONE CENT FOR TRIBUTE   127

spoiled, but salt water will not damage Chinese dishes. They were exquisitely decorated, and today dishes brought from Canton to the Yankee ports in the bilges of tea ships are among the choicest of antiques.)

1 trunk of dry goods. (Doubtless from the hand looms of India. There was no American textile industry then and the calicoes, bandannas and gurrahs of India usually formed part of the cargo of a vessel homeward bound from Calcutta.)

4 mahogany logs and 10 mahogany boards. (From the West Indies and much prized by the makers of fine furniture. Many of the best American antiques are of "San Domingo" mahogany.)

7 barrels of gum benzoin were a product of Sumatra or Java, where grow the trees from which this exotic stuff is produced. It is used as incense and also in the science of medicine as a stimulant and expectorant.

A barrel and a half of sal ammoniac was another medicine brought from the Orient by the Yankee traders, this one being derived from a tree that grows in Persia (now called Iran).

This is the *George Washington*'s cargo of tribute. Added to this list were a couple of items the Americans thought might amuse the barbaric ruler of Algiers. Experience had taught our people that some piece of finery or unusual jewelry or any oddity went far to get these barbarians into a more mellow frame of mind. On this ship our government included five "red birds" and cages and two squirrels and "houses" to provide diversion for the leisure moments of the Dey and his court.

On August 8, 1800, the ship departed from Philadelphia. Her voyage was uneventful. No French privateers were unwise enough to meddle with a vessel carrying fifteen nine-pounders, and no storms delayed her progress, so by September 18, 1800, she arrived at Algiers and commenced unloading. This much of the account of the cruise of the *George Washington* may cause the reader of today to ask if there ever could have been a time when such a government dared tell the United States that its ships might sail in certain waters only by paying for the privilege.

Today a government of the strength of Algiers that presumed to delay the voyage of an American ship by as much as a day would find itself in immediate difficulties and a squadron of our warships would not be long in arriving. Indeed, one recent difficult situation was quickly cleared up soon after units of the United States Navy took blockading stations. In 1800, however, the Turkish Empire was a power in the world. Its territories included all of North Africa to the Atlantic coast of Morocco, and the four Barbary Powers were regencies subordinate to the Sultan at Constantinople. The Turks held the entire Middle East—Syria, Palestine, Persia, Iraq, Arabia, Egypt and the Tigris-Euphrates Valley. Greece was theirs, and much of Yugoslavia, Rumania and Bulgaria.

There had been a time when Spain had been under Mohammedan rule, and the great armies of the Turks besieged Vienna and engaged the Russians in constant border warfare. In 1800 the Barbary States were powers that made many a nation pay tribute; in fact, only Britain and France had the strength to obtain any respect from them. The United States was a weak nation and therefore had to pay.

Let it not be thought that the Americans enjoyed this situation or that they intended to remain weak. William

Eaton, our consul at Tunis, wrote to the Secretary of State, "There is no access to these courts without paving the way either with gold or with cannon balls." Lacking the means of delivering cannon balls, the Americans paid. But in 1794 Congress passed an act providing for the construction of six frigates. Again in 1799 it was enacted that citizens might subscribe funds for more frigates, and another group of men-of-war were built. Several schooners and brigs of war were authorized.

In 1800, however, the American strength was not ready to try conclusions with the Barbary Powers for a very excellent reason: we were engaged in a naval war with France, largely in the West Indies. So the United States Government sent its tribute to Algiers.

When the *George Washington*'s cargo was unloaded at Algiers, preparations made to sail back to the United States were rudely interrupted. The Dey announced that he, in turn, had to pay tribute to the Grand Signor at Constantinople, the Sultan of Turkey. This American man-of-war had arrived at just the right time to perform the task of transportation for him.

This demand came as a terrific blow to the American consul, Richard O'Brien, and to Captain William Bainbridge of the *George Washington,* both of whom engaged in a fierce dispute with the Dey over this order. American protests were useless, for the Dey of Algiers calmly announced that either Bainbridge would transport the cargo for him or American peace with Algiers would be forfeited. And he reminded Bainbridge that his vessel lay within range of the hundreds of guns of the forts of Algiers. Simple it would be to give the command to fire. The American ship would then be sunk, and her crew would become slaves.

Consul O'Brien and Captain Bainbridge, deeply humili-
ated, were forced to agree to do this errand for Algiers. And
then their humiliation was increased. Since the vessel was
to sail on the business of Algiers, said the Dey, the American
flag was to be lowered from the main topgallant masthead
and the Algerian flag was to be hoisted in its place. This
Captain Bainbridge did, and then the castle fired a seven-
gun salute to the Algerian flag now floating above a warship
of the United States Navy.

Bainbridge, in his report to the Secretary of the Navy,
said that his refusal nearly brought about a declaration of
war, which was avoided only when he acceded to the Dey's
demand. His officers felt the disgrace deeply. "Some tears
fell at this instance of national humility," wrote Bainbridge.
He added that an English ship of war had arrived and
offered to carry the Dey's tribute and his embassy to the
Sultan's court, but the Dey did not accept this offer, sup-
posing he would then be under some obligations to the
British.

So on October 20, 1800, the *George Washington* departed
from Algiers for Constantinople, laden with the Dey's cargo
and flying his flag. Humiliating it may have been, however,
Consul O'Brien and Captain Bainbridge had decided wisely
to act to preserve peace. The American merchant marine
was very active in this part of the world. Their cargoes were
valuable, and they were making fortunes for their owners
and a good living for crews and the people of our seaport
towns. To this day many a city along our Atlantic coast is
proud of the mansions built from the profits of our trade
of that era.

The Dey's cargo list, quite different from that on the voyage from Philadelphia to Algiers, deserves examination. First on the list are twenty "gentlemen." These were high-ranking persons in Algiers, an embassy to present the respects of the regency to their sovereign lord, the Grand Signor, Sultan of Turkey. Then appears a group designated as "100 negro Turks," which probably means Negroes who had become Mohammedans. There were also aboard sixty Turkish women, and on these we have no particulars or any hint as to why they were going to Constantinople unless as recruits for the various harems of the city.

Then there appear some entries that were calculated to make life interesting at the Grand Signor's Court: 4 lions and 4 "tygers," 4 antelopes, 12 parrots, some leopards and some ostriches. These creatures must have been brought across the Sahara to Algiers by caravan, for they are all native to the veldt and jungle of central Africa. We can only guess what was meant by "tyger," for that is an animal found only in Asia.

The cargo was completed with jewels, money, 4 horses and 200 sheep. These animals in cages and pens on deck doubtless turned the spick-and-span decks of the American warship into a barnyard. However, our naval officers probably felt that the ordure of two hundred and fifty animals on the deck of their ship was a small burden compared with the humiliation of having the Algerian flag flying at their main topgallant masthead.

The *George Washington* arrived at Constantinople on November 11, 1800, discharged her cargo and lay at anchor while the Algerian embassy of twenty "gentlemen" waited upon the ruler of all the Turkish dominions. Here the Americans were paid considerable attention. The Turkish court had never heard of America, and this was the first vessel flying our national colors ever to visit Constantinople. They had never seen the flag before. The American ship was treated courteously by the Turks during its rather long stay awaiting the time when the Algerian embassy was ready to return.

It was not until December thirtieth that the ship left Constantinople, and then without an important part of the Algerian embassy. However much the officers and crew of the American man-of-war may have fumed and fretted at being ordered to transport a cargo of tribute from Philadelphia to Algiers, and whatever may have been their feeling of humiliation when their ship was forced to convey the Dey's tribute to Constantinople with the Algerian flag flying from her masthead, they now had their satisfaction.

It became plain that most of the Algerian embassy were to remain in Constantinople, while those who came aboard for the return voyage had the dejected look of whipped dogs. Captain Bainbridge was ashore frequently; he was friendly with Capudan Pasha, an important official in the Sultan's Court, and with Lord Elgin, the British ambassador. From them he learned the true story.

Napoleon had conquered Egypt, a possession of the Sultan of Turkey. The British, implacable enemies of Napoleon, ever ready to strike him from any angle whatsoever, had made common cause with the Sultan and were preparing an expedition against Egypt. The British pointed out to the Sultan that his regency of Algiers had recently made a treaty with France and had furthermore captured the ships of various of Britain's allies and had enslaved the sailors.

The Sultan was furious. He detained the most important

members of the embassy from Algeria and gave the others a letter to the Dey, requiring him to declare war upon France at once and to release all captives of nations allied to Britain. So the *George Washington* returned to Algiers with these bearers of bad tidings. Upon reaching Algiers the Americans watched happily to see what effect this news would have upon the ill-tempered and tyrannical ruler of this regency.

The explosion was immediate. This triumph of British diplomacy at Constantinople resulted in an immediate declaration of war against France and the liberation of all captives of nations allied to England. The Dey announced that all French who were not out of the city in two days would be cast into prison in chains.

The United States had only recently settled the naval war with France, and the Dey's threat to the French presented Captain Bainbridge with an opportunity he was quick to grasp. He at once volunteered to take all the French from Algiers. Bainbridge had been fearful the Dey would order the *George Washington* on another mission of some sort. If he took the French away, then his vessel would be free. He could deliver the French at a friendly port and then return to America.

It worked out that way. The French refugees were landed at Alicante in Spain, and at last the *George Washington* headed homeward, her long ordeal over. On April 19, 1801, she reached Philadelphia.

This was not an end to American payments to Algiers or of the *George Washington*'s work in transporting tribute. Again on July 20, 1801, she departed from Philadelphia with a cargo for the Dey. But there were differences this time. The United States Government had taken a serious view of the indignity our flag had suffered when the *George Washington* had been forced to sail to Constantinople flying the Algerian colors. The new captain, John Shaw, was ordered to resist any attempt to send his ship anywhere or to compel her to do anything "derogatory to the honor of the Flag of the United States."

One might ask what Captain Shaw could do to prevent such an outrage when Captain Bainbridge had been powerless. The answer is interesting. His orders were to send for Commodore Dale's squadron. When we concluded our naval war with France, the Navy Department had at its disposal warships to dispatch on a badly needed patrol of the Mediterranean to try to teach the rulers of Barbary better manners.

This squadron, three frigates and a schooner, arrived at Gibraltar too late to help keep the Bashaw of Tripoli in line, for he had declared war on the United States shortly before our ships arrived. Two of Tripoli's raiders, which had set out to capture American merchantmen, were in Gibraltar harbor when our squadron came sailing in. One of our ships was left to blockade them while the others sailed east to conduct operations against Tripoli.

The presence of our squadron gave Captain Shaw perfect insurance against any further outrageous demands from Algiers. The Dey knew the power of the American frigates. He had no desire for a close acquaintanceship. So the second voyage of the *George Washington* was uneventful. She delivered her cargo, returned to Philadelphia, and she passed out of history when the Navy Department sold her for a merchantman.

The story of our relations with the Barbary Powers, however, does not end there. From 1801 to 1805 we fought a war with Tripoli that sometimes involved blockade, sometimes no activity at all and occasionally blazing action. There was always a powerful squadron of American ships in the Mediterranean, so the Dey of Algiers behaved.

As for Tripoli, it was not total victory for the United States, but it was enough of a victory so that the Bashaw became thoroughly tired of war and was glad to sign a treaty of peace. For some years American merchantmen traded up and down the Mediterranean with no interference.

The good behavior of the Barbary Powers, learned as they watched the United States Navy make life miserable for Tripoli, vanished in 1812 when the Americans became involved in war with England. It seemed certain the American navy would be completely wiped out. The British assured them this would happen. So the Barbary States, particularly Algiers, seized what few American ships they could find.

In 1815, the war with England over, the United States Government decided it was time to end forever the piratical practices of the Barbary Powers. The American navy, far from being wiped out, was stronger than before the war. At New York a ten-ship squadron was assembled, Captain Stephen Decatur commanding, and sailed May 20, 1815.

Off the southeastern coast of Spain the Americans caught Algeria's best frigate, reducing it to a wreck in a short and sharp action. Some days later they captured an Algerian brig of war. Then Decatur sailed his squadron into the harbor of Algiers and dictated a peace with his guns covering the city. By the terms of this peace, tribute was forever abolished, American slaves were turned over to the navy and compensation was arranged for American ships captured by Algiers. The squadron then sailed to Tunis and to Tripoli and dealt with them.

As William Eaton had said years before, "There is no access to these courts without paving the way either with gold or with cannon balls." It had taken the Americans a long time to arrange for the delivery of cannon balls, but at last they managed it. The war with Tripoli did a great deal of good, and Decatur's expedition in 1815 completed the work. Never again did any of the Barbary regencies dare trouble an American ship.

11

The End of a Frigate

IN THE AUTUMN of 1803 the American war with Tripoli had been going on for more than two years. It was an uneventful and tedious war, consisting of little more than an American blockade of Tripoli that was enforced at times and at other times completely neglected.

The war, such as it was, had resulted in some advantage to the Americans. At the very outset the U.S.S. *Enterprise*, a schooner commanded by Lieutenant Sterrett and armed with sixteen six-pounders, had administered an unmerciful drubbing to the enemy warship *Tripoli*, carrying eighteen six-pounders. The *Tripoli*'s casualties were heavy; she struck her flag. The Americans threw overboard her cannon, cut down her masts and left her to limp home with a jury mast.

Upon the *Tripoli*'s arrival in port, the Bashaw flew into a rage, ordered her commander given five hundred blows with the bastinado and paraded through the city astride a jackass. Whatever his fit of temper, the lesson of this battle was not lost on the Bashaw. As far as Tripoli was concerned, the Americans ruled the Mediterranean and he knew better than to send out any of his men-of-war against them.

So one good result was that American ships now could sail the Mediterranean without fear of attack by Tripoline corsairs. The United States squadron based at Syracuse saw to that. And some pressure was exerted on Tripoli by the blockade, intermittent and slack as it was. Late in 1803 measures were being taken to tighten the blockade.

The incompetent Commodore Morris, who had commanded the squadron in the first part of 1803, had been removed. In his place was Commodore Edward Preble, as capable and efficient a naval officer as ever served in the United States Navy. He saw to it that one of our ships was on duty off Tripoli as much of the time as was possible.

In October 1803 the frigate *Philadelphia,* commanded by Captain William Bainbridge, patrolled the waters off Tripoli, with the U.S.S. *Vixen,* a schooner, in company. Bainbridge thought it wasteful to keep two warships on the blockade station, so he ordered the smaller and lighter *Vixen* to sail west and cruise off Cape Bon in the hope she might encounter some Tripoline merchantmen in that area, homeward bound and planning to run the blockade at night.

The *Philadelphia* continued to perform the tedious patrol before Tripoli alone. This was a fine thirty-six-gun frigate, built by the private subscription of the people of Philadelphia a few years before, when the government announced that it would welcome any private help it could get in building more ships for the navy. Among those built under this program were the *New York,* the *Boston,* the *John Adams* (at Charleston, S.C.) and the *Essex* (at Salem).

It was on October 31, 1803, five leagues east of Tripoli, that the *Philadelphia*'s masthead lookout saw a vessel skulking along inshore, plainly bound for the harbor. At once the

American frigate commenced the chase and pursued the enemy blockade runner close to the shore, opening fire with her heavy guns. In the *Philadelphia*'s bow were three leadsmen to heave the lead and shout the depth of water, for in a pursuit close to shore there was an active danger the vessel might run into shoal water and go aground.

And the water did begin to shoal. Captain Bainbridge was forced to turn away from shore before he could get near enough to the enemy vessel to reach her with shot from his bow chasers. Coming about, the *Philadelphia* commenced to beat against the easterly breeze, tediously tacking away from the coast.

Available records indicate that the three leadsmen who had been posted in the bow as the ship pursued close inshore were secured when the *Philadelphia* slowly beat out to sea. Indeed, there seemed to be no occasion to have leadsmen in the bow; the chart clearly showed good water all the way out to the open sea.

Then it happened. The frigate struck; her bow encountered some submerged obstacle. She came to a jarring halt, her masts swayed, and she rode up onto a reef of rocks so that her forepart was slightly out of water. Soundings were then taken; there was twelve feet of water forward and seventeen feet aft. The ship had an eighteen-foot draft and she had struck an enormous uncharted rock formation.

Captain Bainbridge wasted not a moment in commencing the procedures for a ship aground. First, he backed all sails in the hope there was enough wind to give her sternway and get her off. That failed. Then the three great anchors in the frigate's bow were cast loose to fall into the sea in foaming splashes. Bainbridge thought that relief from their weight might raise the bow enough to free her. This was not effective.

Then the water was "started"; the bungs were knocked from the many hogsheads of drinking water for the crew, and it was allowed to run overboard. Some of the forward guns were hove overboard, and others were run aft. The foremast was cut down, and when it went by the board it carried away the main topgallant mast.

Still the frigate *Philadelphia* was hard aground, listing so the guns on one side pointed upward a few degrees and the guns on the other side pointed a few degrees down toward the water. The gunboats of Tripoli, a dozen of them, had arrived by this time and were firing. These were small vessels each carrying one eighteen-pounder or a twenty-four-pounder and designed for harbor and coast defense. It took but one look from shore for the Tripolines to see the trouble the American frigate was in. They swarmed around the helpless ship like hyenas around a wounded lion.

The only guns the Americans could bring to bear were the stern chasers, and these they had to put in such an unusual position that the blast from the muzzles set the ship afire. They extinguished the blaze and kept up a fire that punished the Tripoline gunboats, but the enemy promptly moved to positions where they could not be reached by the American stern guns. Quite safe, the Tripoline gunboats stationed themselves beyond the reach of musket fire from the sailors and marines of the *Philadelphia* and proceeded to slug away at the frigate with their eighteen- and twenty-four-pounders. Had the American frigate been on an even keel, she could have swept these gunboats away with a couple of well-aimed broadsides.

Tripoline gunnery was notoriously inaccurate, and one

American frigate could have taken care of any number of such gunboats. For four hours these craft fired from fairly close range. They received no return fire, but with all this cannonading they accomplished little beyond cutting up the *Philadelphia*'s rigging. By the end of the four hours Captain Bainbridge decided that he was endangering the lives of his entire crew without being able to damage the enemy in any way whatsoever. So he surrendered his ship and the American colors slowly came down the halyards until they reached the deck.

A court-martial of Captain William Bainbridge was held after the war was over, the verdict of which was that he had acted with fortitude and was deserving of no censure. His entire staff of officers signed a statement that he had done everything that a good officer should have done. There are officers who do their duty beyond possibility of censure. Such a one was Bainbridge. Then there are great officers who come through the most trying and difficult situations victoriously. Such a one we will hear about presently.

Bainbridge was exonerated, and yet we wonder why a captain so close inshore on a strange coast, where charts are made by persons whose competence is doubtful, should be sailing blithely along without his leadsmen in the bow. We wonder what some other captain might have managed to do with the *Philadelphia*'s big guns even though the vessel lay canted at such an angle. And what would have happened had he held out until darkness? There are captains who would have conducted a small-boat attack on the gunboats and carried some of them, or who would have led an escape of the crew in the boats and destroyed the frigate.

Fruitless speculations, these, nor would we indulge in

them did we not recall the deeds of some of the other officers of the United States Navy, both in this and in a later day. What did actually happen was that the entire American crew was carried off into captivity in Tripoli after being robbed of every object of the slightest value, including some of the clothing they were wearing.

Two days following the surrender of the frigate a strong westerly gale came up. Seeing their opportunity, the Tripoline gunboats put lines on the *Philadelphia,* and with the help of the strong wind and the waves they were able to haul her off the rock. Then they located on the bottom of the sea the guns which had been hove overboard, raised them and put them back on board. The frigate was towed to an anchorage near the walls of the Bashaw's castle, so that he could admire this man-of-war that was now his, a finer vessel than he ever imagined would fly his flag. Here she lay, ready, when refitted, to sail forth to teach these Americans a lesson. And then, in moments when the prowess of his mariners seemed somewhat doubtful to him, the Bashaw played with the idea of selling his frigate to Algiers or Tunis or Morocco.

The officers and men entered upon a long, dreary and tedious captivity. The only one of the American crew who had any interesting experiences was Dr. Jonathan Cowdery, surgeon of the frigate. This we know because he kept a journal which, fortunately, has been preserved.

The robbery of the American prisoners, when nearly complete, was halted by a group of Tripoline officers who attacked their own men with sabres. According to Dr. Cowdery, these officers cut off the hands of some of the thieves and were said to have killed others. He was shocked by this bloodthirsty manner of preserving a few shreds of propriety, although these thieving rapscallions had rifled his pockets, stolen his case of surgical instruments and had even taken the handkerchief from around his neck.

In Tripoli the American prisoners were closely confined, and the only aid given them came from Nicholas Nissen, the Danish consul. He extended them credit, obtained decent food for the sick, transmitted letters to the outside world and performed all manner of friendly services. Three of the American sailors managed to find a way of ending their captivity. Following the maxim, "If you can't lick them, join them," they "turned Turk," became Mohammedans and expressed the wish to enlist in the forces of the Bashaw of Tripoli. One of these, John Wilson, was made an overseer in charge of the American prisoners. He later appeared on a Navy list of "Wanted" men and all of our men-of-war were instructed to keep an eye out for him. He never was apprehended, but had he been, it is fairly certain he would have graced the yardarm of some United States man-of-war.

The reason life in Tripoli was more interesting for Dr. Cowdery than for the other prisoners was that the Bashaw decided it would be well to try the services of an American doctor. The local physicians had strange potions like elixir of camel's urine and various incantations and procedures grounded in Oriental magic. On December 5, 1803, the Bashaw sent for Dr. Cowdery to prescribe for him and two officers of his bodyguard. His journal under the date of December 6 records that upon his visit he found his patients improved.

At this same time one of the ministers asked him to prescribe for a blindness in the left eye. Cowdery wrote in his journal: "I prescribed for him with very little success."

Calls at the palace to treat ailing officials became more frequent. On January 1, 1804, he attended the Bashaw's eleven-months-old child, who was dangerously ill. He was able to help the baby, and the grateful Bashaw offered the doctor a horse and a servant so that he might ride in the countryside.

On February third the Bashaw was ill and sent for Dr. Cowdery. The journal describes the procedure of getting to the Bashaw's presence. He had to pass several sentinels, then he was escorted through a pack of fifty fiercely yelping dogs and through three heavily bolted iron doors which were opened by armed mamelukes. Our Navy surgeon apparently knew his business, for on February sixth a very much improved Bashaw sent for Dr. Cowdery to come to the castle. He shook hands with the doctor, received him with great politeness and requested him to become his family physician.

On February 16, 1804, Dr. Cowdery's position as family physician was further strengthened when he was called to attend the Bashaw's eldest daughter, a married woman. He must have done well, for his journal records that her husband offered the good doctor many civilities.

These were the last civilities Dr. Cowdery or any other American prisoner received for a very long time. The journal records: "At five o'clock P.M. we were informed that two English merchantmen were standing in for the harbor. They proved, however, to be two vessels under the command of Captain Decatur. About eleven P.M., we were alarmed by a most hideous yelling and screaming from one end of the town to the other and a firing of cannon from the castle. On getting up and opening the window which faced the harbor, we saw the frigate *Philadelphia* in flames."

There, in a simple diary entry, is the story of what happened toward midnight on February 16, 1804. The Americans had slipped into the very heart of this stronghold of Barbary power and in one short, sharp fight they had destroyed this frigate of theirs, captive to an alien race.

We see this from where Dr. Cowdery stood, a big fire on the water front, and continuing in his journal, we read of the consternation in Tripoli, troops coming and going, extra guards at the doors of the American prisoners, closer confinement for these navy men. And in the hearts of Captain Bainbridge and his men was a secret joy that their ship no longer existed and her decks were no longer to be profaned by enemy feet.

How did this come to pass? On the frigate *Constitution*, flagship of the Mediterranean squadron, lying in the harbor at Syracuse in the island of Sicily, Commodore Edward Preble had been planning ever since that day more than three months before when first he heard of the capture of the frigate *Philadelphia*. Preble was a man accustomed to having his plans bring results. His squadron and the entire United States Navy as well were disgraced by the capture of one of its ships, practically intact, by this piratical rabble. Preble vowed he would take no peace until this disgrace to him and his squadron and the navy he served was wiped out.

He looked about him for means and he found at hand a Mediterranean rigged ketch captured recently from her Tripoline crew. Named *Mastico*, he promptly ordered that she be called henceforth the U.S.S. *Intrepid*.

A good commander knows his men. In his cabin, seated at the long oval mahogany table, Preble ran over in his mind the names of the young officers in his command. He was not long in making his choice for a desperate mission: Stephen Decatur. He sent for him and explained what he wanted done. Shortly afterward Decatur reported to Preble that he had a crew of volunteers and was ready to sail.

With the brig of war *Siren* in company, the *Intrepid* put out for Tripoli, arriving in the outer harbor several days later at night. A rising storm, however, made it impossible to enter. For days they ran before the blow, and then they had to sail tediously back to Tripoli.

The *Intrepid* arrived first, with the *Siren* not far behind, but Decatur decided he could not wait for his consort, lest the time of darkness slip by or the wind give out. With most of his men concealed below and those on deck disguised as Maltese mariners, Decatur's *Intrepid* sailed slowly into the port of Tripoli, guided by his Maltese pilot, Salvador Catalano.

"Remember," whispered Decatur to his men, "we attack alone because the *Siren* with this light wind can never get into the harbor in time. The fewer the number the greater the honor. The watchword is *Philadelphia*."

Cutlasses, pikes and tomahawks were now issued to the men, with strict orders that there was to be no firing. Barely moving with the faint breeze, the ketch passed under the guns of Fort American and Mandrach and the Maltese Castle. From ashore came no sound. Closer and closer toward the city sailed the *Intrepid,* and for all anyone ashore could tell, she was just another little trader making port, laden with wheat or fish.

At a whispered order the men climbed out of the hatchway and crawled over into the dark shadow of the bulwarks. Barely moving, the ketch neared the *Philadelphia.* The masts and spars and shrouds of the frigate towered above them in a symmetrical pattern against the starlit sky. Suddenly from the deck above came a loud hail, followed by a string of Arabic words. Salvador Catalano replied that the vessel had lost its anchors in the storm and asked if they could tie up alongside.

From the deck above came more shouted Arabic, and permission was granted. Then, when the Americans were within a few yards of the frigate, the faint wind died altogether. The *Intrepid,* her way checked, drifted like a piece of flotsam, where one broadside could reduce her to a mass of wreckage.

Catalano and two of the American crew slid down a line to a small boat in tow astern. Slowly they rowed around to the bow, took a cable passed to them through the *Intrepid*'s starboard hawse hole and then, as deliberately as if they had all night, they sculled ahead to meet another cable brought out to them by two swarthy sailors from the *Philadelphia.* When the two lines were fastened together, Catalano and the two sailors, still undetected in their disguises, pulled back to the *Intrepid* with leisurely strokes and climbed aboard.

The cable lay slack along the *Intrepid*'s deck; it drooped from the hawse hole, floated limply in the water and ran up the frigate's side and over the bulwarks to her anchor bitts, where it was made fast. At a low-voiced order the crowd of men hidden in the shadows laid hold of the hawser, put their backs into it and gave way. The heavy line came out of the water with a snap, taut and dripping. The astounded sentry gaped at this strange craft, which a moment before had been becalmed and now moved ahead like a live thing.

Before he could sense what was happening, the *Intrepid* ranged alongside, scraping against the frigate's side planking

with a heavy thud. Now the sentry saw the long pikes and
glinting cutlass blades of the men swarming on the deck below. His voice caught in his throat and he fired his musket,
screaming:

"Americanos. Americanos."

Shouting wildly, some of the Tripoline crew ran to cut
the hawser while others dashed for the muskets and scimitars
in the racks at the foot of the mainmast. The watch below
came tumbling out of their hammocks at the sound of the
uproar and the pounding feet on the deck over their heads,
but they were too late.

The sharp hooks of the grappling irons already bit into
the wood of the bulwarks. The Americans swarmed up the
rope ladders, and with Decatur in the lead, they hacked down
the Tripolines who rushed to the rail to repel boarders. Then
the *Intrepid's* men were on deck, pikes thrusting, cutlass
blades and tomahawks flashing.

The tide of battle swiftly receded toward the forecastle,
where the Bashaw's sailors, beaten and cornered, were diving
overboard and sliding down the anchor cables. The fight was
over. Of the enemy who still lived, some swam for the nearby
shore, and others made off in a boat. Quickly men were sent
below to break open the magazine, while on deck Midshipman Izard stood with a flaming torch in each hand. Their
work done, the men came up from below.

"All hands abandon ship," roared Decatur.

Over the side climbed the *Intrepid's* crew, pikes and cutlasses clattering to the deck below, and down they went over
the ladders and ropes, leaping the last few feet to the ketch.

"Heave your torches," shouted Decatur to Izard.

As the torches arched through the air and down the hatch,

leaving a trail of sparks and smoke, Decatur and Izard leaped for the side of the ship and were over, sliding down the lines to the deck below. The light of the torches was gone, and for an instant there was complete blackness. Then came the explosion, a churning, rolling wave of fire pushing far up into the rigging in a white-hot gale, carrying with it fragments of plank and boards and barrel staves that formed black specks in the blinding glare.

The incandescent column of fire towered higher than the masts. Above the flames streamed a million sparks and a great rolling cloud of gray smoke. The forts, castles and stone buildings of the city and the ships in the harbor stood out in every smallest detail in the scarlet light. Repeated explosions shook the *Philadelphia*. Blasts spouted up from the vitals of the ship; red-hot embers showered down, sizzling into the water, charring the deck of the *Intrepid* and dropping on the men, searing their skin.

The crew cut the cable and with their heavy sweeps they fended off from the burning frigate. They set the sweeps in the thole pins, and the blades bit water as the men bent their backs to the rowing. It was none too soon, for the *Intrepid*'s paint was blistering in the heat and the tar in the seams of the deck planking bubbled and ran. With seventy men at the sweeps, the ketch gathered way, and the heat lessened noticeably.

But now the *Intrepid,* well away from the burning frigate, stood outlined in the light of the fire, a plain target for every gun along the entire harbor front. All the cannon in Tripoli flashed and thundered. From the forts, the Bashaw's castle and the vessels of their navy they fired at the little ketch slowly making out of the harbor. By the light of the blazing

ship the waters glowed red, and the people crowded piers
and roof tops to watch their powerful batteries sink this little
vessel that had brought the enemy colors under the very walls
of the Bashaw's castle.

Round shot screamed and chattered over the *Intrepid,*
plunging into the sea everywhere about her. Fountains of
water towered and splashed, some close aboard, showering
the men with spray, more at a safe distance, far from the
little craft. Even the guns of the *Philadelphia,* kept loaded
and shotted to meet a sudden attack, were now fired by the
heat of the blaze and joined in the cannonade.

A shot pierced the *Intrepid*'s mainsail, opening a wide
hole. Another skimmed across the taffrail, showering the
helmsman with splinters. A man at the sweeps felt a sudden
wind above him and his cap flew off. Midshipman Morris
picked it up and clapped it back on the man's head.

"Closest yet," he said. "If that ball had been a foot lower,
I'd have the nasty job of picking up your head. Pull, man,
pull."

Finally they got beyond the range of the guns. The Bashaw's gunners, having made a more thunderous and soul-
satisfying uproar than the city had heard in its entire history,
felt that they had done well. Yet not one damaging hit had
they scored on the American man-of-war. Few among the
Tripoline artillerymen had the slightest idea of laying and
aiming a cannon. Noise, smoke, the flash of the gun—this they
thought was war, and tedious calculations and sightings of
the piece were the silly ideas of schoolmasters. So they did not
hit their target, growing constantly smaller in the increasing
distance.

Then from the frigate *Philadelphia* came a greater explo-

sion. Burning timbers hurtling aloft left fiery trails, and hot
molten copper spikes arched into the sky in a glowing green
tracery. The deck heaved upward, and the blazing masts
canted over, sinking slowly toward the water. Ashore the people ran to escape the shower of burning wreckage.

The fire died down and the clouds of smoke, gradually
thinning, slowly moved away across the sky. Here and there
planks and timbers still glowed, dropping one by one into
the water. Darkness fell upon the harbor which only moments before had been as brightly lighted as a stage.

The frigate was no more. The timber, the cordage, the
iron, gathered from the states of the American Union, lov-
ingly fitted together into the fabric of a ship and given a
proud name, lay scattered along the African shore, now mere
flotsam. The ship had at last died with honor.

Three days after the furious battle in Tripoli harbor the
Intrepid sighted Sicily. It was dawn; far ahead the pink of
first light lay on Mt. Etna's snow-covered peak. Along the
northern horizon the land was purple, and as the ketch sailed
through the early-morning hours, the dark hills took on the
fresh green of springtime. The towers and white stone buildings and red roofs of Syracuse stood out more clearly now.

Lieutenant Decatur, telescope to his eye, took a sight on
the columns of the ancient Greek temple and gave the helmsman his course. Sweeping the vessels in the harbor, his gaze
paused at the mizzen gaff halyards of the *Constitution*, where
signal pennants whipped in the breeze. His lips formed letters as he read, and he smiled.

Decatur spoke to his officers in an exultant voice that carried forward, for he meant that every man aboard should hear.

"Gentlemen, the flagship signals the question, 'Have you

succeeded?' Midshipman Izard, you will hoist the affirmative pennant, if you please."

Slowly the *Intrepid* sailed into the harbor, gradually nearing the flagship *Constitution*. Then, when they were no more than a cable's length distant, an officer aboard the big frigate whipped out an order. Instantly the crew sprang into the rigging, over three hundred men, all in dress uniform.

Up the ratlines they climbed, out along the foreyard and main and mizzen, more of them higher to the topsail yards, to the topgallants and royals. Up forward, others worked out on the bowsprit and the jib boom; some took positions in the fighting tops, a few along the forecastle head. When all had stopped moving, neatly spaced lines of men were ranged along every spar on the ship, holding to lifts and braces and the headsail rigging.

The entire crew, gunners and topmen and petty officers, marines and cooks and powder monkeys, stood motionless and at attention in the evolution of manning the yards, an honor given only to those who have deserved well of their country. Ensigns, jacks, blue and red and yellow signal flags, even the Commodore's broad pendant, fluttered at every peak and halyard, dressing ship for the men of the *Intrepid*.

Another order snapped out. Every man drew in a deep breath, and a mighty cheer rolled over the harbor, then another and a third. The crews of the smaller *Enterprise* and *Vixen,* aloft to man their rigging, gave their own roaring welcome to the men who had destroyed America's captive frigate. The cruise of the *Intrepid* was ended, her mission accomplished.

But the career of her commander had only begun. Given one of the most difficult tasks in our naval history, he had executed it skillfully. Some would say fortune favored him, yet events of later years were to prove in his case that fortune has a way of smiling on the man who has worked and thought to be prepared in all ways and who makes the most of every situation without ever giving up while there remains one more move he can make. Thus did the disgraceful capture of the frigate at last end in glorious victory.

12

Midshipman Wadsworth

NOWHERE IN NAVAL HISTORY does there appear an instance of a small navy with so outstanding a record as that of the Americans in the early days of the Republic. There was ample opportunity, for those were days of uncertainty, conflict, vast power struggles; times when men, and nations, lived dangerously. Americans realized that a nation unwilling to live dangerously might, before long, not be living at all.

Three times in those early days was America in naval conflict with the enemy. It took a good part of the years 1799 and 1800 to teach French privateers and the navy itself that it is unrewarding to prey upon American merchant vessels. Hardly had this lesson been completed than it became necessary to conduct similar instruction for the benefit of the Bashaw of Tripoli, who had persisted in the notion that the Stars and Stripes flew at the mizzen gaff halyards of the vessels of a weak nation. Tripoli was a stubborn foe, and the war continued from 1801 to 1805 before the American navy made the Mediterranean safe for our commerce.

The third and last of our wars fought for the freedom of the seas was with mighty Britain. Commencing in 1812, it was marked by many a dark moment for the United States, then a nation sparsely populated, not wealthy and without an army capable of standing up to trained troops. Our navy was very small compared with the vast English fleet. Our coasts were blockaded, our merchant fleet was forced to stay in port, and the enemy landed where he pleased on our coast.

Yet when the United States Navy met the British on equal terms, the results were astonishing, and victory usually resulted. Red-faced Englishmen everywhere clawed about for some explanation of the continual defeat of their proud men-of-war by the vessels of their upstart rebel cousins across the sea. The explanations, which were not very good, never once mentioned the real reason: the outstanding quality of the American ships and the men who sailed them.

In what they did rather than in what they said may we read what the Lords of the Admiralty really thought of the United States Navy. The order went out that no British frigate was to engage an American frigate alone; they were to sail in pairs. No greater compliment has ever been paid the United States Navy.

One great factor in the success of any naval or military force is the quality of the officer corps. Our navy's doctrine created an excellent group of officers; names such as Edward Preble, Stephen Decatur, Isaac Hull, David Porter, Andrew Sterett and Oliver Hazard Perry live in history, and this is to mention but a few of the many from the earliest days who later distinguished themselves. For every one who is remembered today and memorialized in textbooks and biographies, there were dozens of hard-working officers who did their duty, led their men, faced danger without flinching, and yet no turn of fortune's wheel ever placed them where they had their day of glory and everlasting distinction.

To such men, unremembered, was due a vast part of American naval success. No brilliant captain, such as Decatur or Hull, can win victory without the backing of the hundreds who give that last ounce toward doing their duty. Henry Wadsworth, a midshipman who joined the frigate *Congress* in 1799, is an example of such a man—little known or written of, but typical. Most of the information about him is tucked away in brief passages in the naval records.

Young Wadsworth received his warrant bearing the signature of the President, and he put on his uniform consisting of a six-button blue coat with a diamond of gold lace on the standing collar, white vest, white breeches and a cocked hat with gold lace. Aboard the frigate the dozen midshipmen studied under the ship's schoolmaster, who was the chaplain. They learned naval tactics from the officers and they were always aloft when sail was being made or taken in. Also, in accordance with naval regulations, each kept a journal.

It is from Henry Wadsworth's journal that we are able to learn so much about him and about life in the old navy. He had an excellent literary style, so his writings are much more interesting than the logbook style of most seafaring men. In the war with France it was not his good fortune to get into action, for his vessel did not meet the enemy's important ships. The *Constitution* and the *Constellation* each met a French frigate, and battle followed. The French vessels in both instances were vanquished, and the crews of the American ships, particularly the young officers, felt they were really beginning to live.

Henry Wadsworth had to content himself with the thought he had done his duty, thus progressing toward the day when he might receive his commission as an officer. Nearly three years were to pass before there was again to be any hope of naval action, the dream of every young naval officer who thought some day to distinguish himself. Then Wadsworth was sent to the Mediterranean squadron engaged in the war against Tripoli.

There he joined the frigate *Chesapeake* at Malta, and on January 31, 1803, his ship departed, the *John Adams* and *New York* in company, to patrol off Tripoli and blockade that port. They ran into a gale and Wadsworth's journal gives this detail of life aboard: "The deck over my cot leaks very much. Of course, my bed and bedding are much wet as the element water is continually in boisterous weather washing over the Gun Deck. At twelve my friend Cram will turn out to keep his watch, when I will turn into his cot, which hangs in a dry place."

This gale was of such violence that the American vessels had to return to Valletta, the port of the island of Malta. Crews given shore leave were not idle, for the next entry in the journal records a duel fought between Midshipman Bainbridge of the U.S.S. *New York* and Mr. Cochran, an Englishman who was secretary to the governor of Malta. This murderous affair was fought at four paces and Cochran "received the ball in his head and instantly died." Duels, often arising from minor provocations, were one of the curses of that age. Although authorities tried to put an end to these affairs that resulted in the death of so many valuable men, it was years before it was possible to stamp out the ridiculous notions of honor that led to the fights.

In another passage Wadsworth mentions a duel in which a lieutenant of his ship was wounded by a captain of marines.

Nowhere is there any reference to a duel in which Henry
Wadsworth himself engaged. This permits us to assume he
had better sense than to become involved in these senseless
combats.

When the weather moderated sufficiently, the *Chesapeake*
sailed with her consorts to patrol off the coast of Tripoli. In
February she was sent to visit Algiers, doubtless to keep the
ruler of that regency more friendly by letting him see the
double row of guns in the broadside of an American frigate.
A passage in the midshipman's journal is very helpful in
giving an idea of life aboard a warship in enemy waters by
supplying a detailed description of an unusual event.

Under the date of April 2, 1803, he writes; "On the 22d
February it being the day after we left Algiers; Mrs. Low
(wife to James Low Captain of the Forecastle) bore a Son,
in the Boatswain's Store Room: On the 31st March the babe
was baptiz'd in the midshipmen's apartment: The Contriver
of this business was Melancthon Taylor Woolsey a Mid: who
stood Godfather on the occasion & provided a handsome col-
lation of Wine & Fruit: Mrs. Low being unwell Mrs. Hays
the Gunner's Lady officiated: Divine Service by Rev. Alex
McFarlan. The Childs name Melancthon Woolsey Low:—
All was conducted with due decorum and decency no doubt
to the great satisfaction of the parents, as Mr. Woolsey's attention to them must in some measure have ameliorated the
unhappy situation of the Lady who was so unfortunate as to
concieve & bare on the Salt Sea. NB. The other ladies of
the Bay—The Forward Most part of the Birth Deck—viz.
Mrs. Watson, the Boatswain's Wife, Mrs. Myres the Carpenter's Lady—with Mrs. Crosby the corporal's Lady: got drunk
in their own Quarters out of pure spite—not being invited

to celebrate the Christening of Melancthon Woolsey Low."

That petty officers could have their wives aboard ship in time of war will astonish most of those who think they know something of naval history. How Midshipman Wadsworth could be sure the lady "concieved" on the salt sea may be questioned by some. Although he refers to the "Birth" deck as the place of residence of these "ladies," he probably was aware that the correct spelling is "berth."

Not long after he was transferred to the *New York,* where at last he was fortunate enough to see action. On May 22, 1803, they bombarded a Tripolitan fort. On May 24 they were in the harbor, but there was no activity. "No fun," he wrote in his journal. On the twenty-seventh, when nine enemy gunboats and one ship were seen "close in with the land," the *New York* opened fire.

"It was now just dusk," he wrote, "and we could no longer discern our enemies but by the flash of their guns: had their been anyone on board who like Joshua of Old could have commanded the sun to stand still, Thy Gun Boats would have been ours, Tripoly, and thy people our Slaves."

Wadsworth found that he had chosen the right profession, if we may judge from the lines that follow:

"It was a most elegant sight, the frequent flash and heavy reports of the gunboats: the still more frequent broad Sides of our squadron form'd the most sublime scene you can imagine. The shot from the Gun boats whistl'd over us and struck all around—but none hit us."

This action was inconclusive, serving only to show the Tripolitans how closely they were blockaded. On June 2, 1803, at a beach thirty-five miles northwest of Tripoli, the Americans launched a small boat attack against a dozen small

grain ships near shore and set fire to them. Wadsworth par-
ticipated, thoroughly enjoying the whole action, including
the enemy's musket fire.

Ashore a thousand Tripolitans fired and demonstrated
wildly, yet did little damage to those in the American cutters
and launches. One warrior on a black horse galloped along
the beach, "flourishing his carbine in defiance," wrote Wadsworth. "Several took aim at him; he plunged forward, fell
and bit the dust."

The frigate *Adams* fired with her twelve-pounders at the
enemy on the beach "excellently well, whenever three or four
were seen running together. If they were not cut down, the
sand would so cover them that for a minute you could not see
them till at last the headmost one would make his appearance
following by the others making haste for the first place of
safety. 'Twas good sport I must confess, yet they might with
justice join the Frogs in the Fable and say what is pleasure
to you is death for us."

Plainly a young man of sensitivity. He had a moment of
feeling sorry for the enemy who were under fire from the
frigate's twelve-pounders. However, even under cannon fire,
the Tripolitans managed to put out the fires set by the Americans on the grain ships and save vessels and cargoes. Wadsworth did not return empty-handed from this raid; he writes
that he brought off an earthen jug with a long neck and two
handles from one of the enemy boats.

Following this indecisive battle, Henry Wadsworth was
transferred to the frigate *Constitution*. In September of 1803
the ship was at Gibraltar, from which port he wrote his
cousin, Nancy Doane, a missive which must have caused some
commotion in his native Portland if the young lady chose to

read it to friends about town.

"We have twelve Moorish officers aboard" [from the regency of Morocco] "Ibrahim Louverais, a princely fellow, invites me (after the war) to go home to Sallee with him and says he will give me four wives."

It was in February of 1804 that the young midshipman must have thought that Fate had decreed he was not to have any more opportunity for real action. Commodore Preble, commander of the American squadron and a great naval officer, planned an expedition by night into the harbor of Tripoli to destroy the captive frigate *Philadelphia*. A small vessel captured from the Tripolitans was to be used, and Stephen Decatur was put in command. Volunteers were called for, and Midshipman Wadsworth was one of those accepted to be in the crew of the ketch, renamed *Intrepid* by the Americans. But when she sailed on her mission in early February of 1804, he was ill, in his bed, there to remain until the middle of March. While the frigate *Constitution* and the other ships of the American squadron manned the yards as the valiant *Intrepid* came into the harbor of Syracuse, signaling the complete success of her mission, Midshipman Henry Wadsworth lay below in his bunk, a sick man, not able even to participate in the welcome to the vessel he should have been aboard.

But later his opportunity came. Commodore Preble formed a plan to close in on Tripoli to give their fleet of gunboats, the Bashaw's castle and the town a real working over. He managed to borrow from the King of Naples six gunboats, each carrying a twenty-four-pounder and two bomb vessels, each with a thirteen-inch sea mortar. His squadron was now composed of these small bombardment vessels, the frigate

Constitution and the sloops of war *Siren, Argus, Vixen, Nautilus, Enterprise* and *Scourge.*

Tripoli had ten gunboats, two galleys, one brig and two schooners. Preble was determined to wipe them out. On August 3, 1804, he launched a thunderous attack which resulted in the capture of three and the sinking of two of the enemy vessels. In this action Lieutenant Trippe of Gunboat Number Six received eleven wounds. On August seventh the action was resumed, and now Henry Wadsworth, promoted to the rank of lieutenant, commanded Gunboat Number Six.

In this and following days of furious battle the town and the forts were given a terrific pounding by the gunboats and the guns of the squadron. The remaining vessels of Tripoli's navy, however, managed to survive by taking a position in the innermost part of the harbor behind a reef.

Preble calculated that after the pounding Tripoli had taken one final sledge-hammer blow might do damage that would break the Bashaw's will, cause him to surrender and yield up the crew of the *Philadelphia,* now in his dungeons, as well as make a treaty not to molest American commerce. His plan was soon in progress. He converted the ketch *Intrepid,* the little vessel Decatur had used to destroy the frigate *Philadelphia,* into a fire ship or an "infernal," to use the language of that day.

Into the hold of the *Intrepid* was placed 15,000 pounds of gunpowder, lying loosely in the hold, and 250 thirteen-inch fused shells. A train of powder was laid from the bow and from the stern. The plan was to work the ketch into the harbor in the darkness to a position close to the Tripolitan navy's anchorage and the walls of the Bashaw's castle, then light the powder train, abandon ship and escape in small boats. The resulting explosion was expected to destroy the enemy's navy and cave in the walls of the castle.

Volunteers were called for. Commodore Preble received a note from Lieutenant Wadsworth as follows: "Mr. Wadsworth informs the Commodore that he wishes to Volunteer his service on board the Infernal destined for the Harbour of Tripoly. H. Wadsworth."

On September 4, 1804, the plans were complete and the *Intrepid* set sail, commanded by Lieutenant Somers, with Lieutenant Wadsworth, Midshipman Israel and ten men. The *Argus, Vixen* and *Nautilus* convoyed her as far as the rocks, and then the *Intrepid* went on alone into the blackness of the moonless night with an easterly breeze filling her sails. But the night was not dark enough to conceal the *Intrepid* wholly, and several shots were fired at her from the batteries of the town.

Suddenly, before she reached her target area, the little vessel blew up with a gigantic explosion. The whole harbor, the town and the sea and land beyond Tripoli were illumined. The populace shrieked in terror. The fused shells arched through the air and fell, some on the forts and in the town, some in the water. Then all was darkness.

The American warships detailed to wait for the *Intrepid*'s men stayed on station until sunrise, but they saw nothing of the ketch, nor did they see anywhere on the face of the waters the two boats in which Somers, Wadsworth, Israel and their men had planned to escape. One of the Tripolitan gunboats had vanished; three others were beached in a badly damaged condition. From that day to this naval people have speculated as to what really happened in the few moments before the greatest explosion the Mediterranean had ever seen.

Some theorized that Tripoli's gunboats had moved to attack the *Intrepid,* boarded her in overwhelming force, and that her determined crew then touched flame to the powder trains, destroying their ship and themselves so the gunpowder would not fall into enemy hands. There is some evidence that the men had made a mutual resolve to blow themselves up rather than let the powder be captured. Tripoli was running perilously short of gunpowder, and the 15,000 pounds aboard the *Intrepid* would have enabled them to redouble their fire at the attacking American squadron.

Another possibility is that the batteries scored a hit on the *Intrepid* with hot shot. In one of the attacks by the squadron, one of our gunboats was destroyed when a hot shot struck the magazine. The vessel blew up with heavy loss of life.

Whichever theory was correct, the *Intrepid* and her men were gone. They had distinguished themselves in their own day and for as long as men will gather to tell stories about the United States Navy. The gallant young Lieutenant Wadsworth from Portland, the youth with the sensitive perception and the facile pen, was gone and his shipmates missed him.

Commodore Preble wrote a handsome tribute to all three of his officers. Congress, on March 3, 1805, passed a resolution of regret. "Their names," said the resolution, "ought to live in the recollections and affections of a grateful country and their conduct ought to be regarded as an example to future generations."

The Wadsworth family of Portland, Maine, received the resolution of Congress memorializing their gallant and debonair youth who had gone out from his home and his town to serve his country and meet death with a smile in faraway Africa. They mourned for him, but it was his sister, Zilpah, married to Stephen Longfellow, who found a way of keeping green the memory of her beloved brother far better than she ever was to know.

She was expecting a child, and when her time came, it was a boy. She named him for her brother, and this boy was christened Henry Wadsworth Longfellow. Young Midshipman Wadsworth had a way with words, as his journal bears evidence. And a way with words, as time went on, was certainly very much a characteristic of the lad who bore his name.

13 ~~~⤳

The Turtle Feast

ON A SAND BAR along the coast of the West India island of Antigua, one bright morning in 1803, lay dozing a huge sea turtle, four feet long with a beam of perhaps three feet. It was slumbering peacefully, with no fear, for there was no creature in these waters that dared trouble it. Its shell was a protective coat of armor, and the bite from the jaws of its hooked beak could crush whatever it fastened upon.

While the powerful leviathan slept, three of the islanders, barefooted and swarthy, sneaked quietly toward it over the sands, not making a sound. When they reached it, all three seized one edge of its shell, gave a vast heave, and the great turtle was now on its back, pawing fiercely and completely helpless.

The islanders got their dugout canoe, beached at a distance, and paddled to the point on the sand bar nearest the turtle. Sliding it along on its back, carefully avoiding its claws and the great snapping beak that could tear a chunk from leg, arm or belly as big as the two fists of a man, they got it near their canoe. Another lift, straining muscles rippling under copper-colored skin, and they managed to get the monster off the sand and into the canoe, still upside down and thrashing about wildly.

Once they had the creature amidships, they commenced a difficult piece of navigation. Across the sea they paddled their craft through the choppy whitecaps. Over the bow came sheets of spray as the boat met each wave, but these three men paid no attention. They were completely intent on keeping their canoe in perfect trim, for if it listed to port or starboard, their prize would slide over the side to disappear in the depths of the Caribbean.

These men knew exactly where they were headed. A Yankee ship in port, particularly a Salem ship, always meant a ready market for anyone smart enough and lucky enough to catch a West India turtle. A Salem ship now lay at anchor in the roadstead. For these islanders, if they kept their canoe on an even keel, this meant hard money from the captain, then luxuries for their families in their cabins ashore and a roaring good time for a while.

They managed to reach the harbor with the turtle still aboard and eased alongside the Yankee vessel. They hailed the deck, and the man standing the anchor watch, when he saw what they had, immediately sent for the captain. Then a bargain was struck, but no coin changed hands until a sling on the end of a line from the main yardarm was lowered to the canoe and the turtle was hoisted to the deck. With the great creature safe on board, still upside down, the transaction was complete; the natives were paid and they departed joyfully with their money, giving voice in one of the songs of the Indies.

Not until this ship was warped into her berth at Derby Wharf in Salem, weeks later, were there further events in this sea monster's existence. An arriving ship always attracts a crowd, even in the busy Salem of the very early 1800s, when one hundred and eighty ships hailed from this town. The wharf was lined with people. In no time they spotted the huge turtle, and the news quickly spread up and down the water front.

The captain knew he would not have to wait long for a customer, perhaps more than one, and then there might be lively bidding. His owner, seeing the turtle as soon as he came aboard after the docking of the ship, had ordered it to be sold to the highest bidder.

Salem was a prosperous place in those days, in population sixth in the United States, and in per capita wealth it was said by some to be the first. The successful merchants lived very well. They had mansions along Chestnut, Federal and Essex Streets and in Washington Square, unequaled anywhere in the country. And these Salem merchants had everything a wealthy person usually has, including the desire to entertain in a kingly fashion.

No entertainment in this town, not even a dance in Hamilton Hall with its superb mirrors and spring floor, could surpass a Salem turtle feast. These took place at a time like this, when a vessel arrived from the West Indies with one of the enormous creatures aboard, on his back and quite unaware of how near he was to fulfilling his ultimate destiny.

Sometimes a turtle feast was staged by one of the important families of Salem, such as the Crowninshields, the Derbys, Forresters, Pickmans, or Billy Gray. Or it might be that one of the clubs or societies of the town would give the party. This turtle was bid in by the East India Marine Society, whose chairman of entertainment had some time ago decided it was time for some activity.

The East India Marine Society which acquired title to the monster from the sands of Antigua was no ordinary club. The members were all deep-water mariners. Only those who had rounded either Cape Horn or the Cape of Good Hope might belong. These were careful shipmasters who recorded in a duplicate logbook every uncharted rock or reef or island they saw in the far oceans of the world, and these logbooks they filed with the society at the end of the voyage. In them were written many strange things, for wherever a member might sail, he observed and made notes. An odd bird or animal, the disposition of a native sultan, interesting tools, the location of French or British men-of-war, changed conditions of trade or of climate or ocean currents, an epidemic of cholera or yellow jack, all were dutifully reported.

So it was that a Salem shipmaster had fewer unpleasant surprises on his voyages. At the rooms of his society, amid the hundreds of specimens and curios brought back by those who had gone before, he could read, listen to other captains and prepare. Most of the merchants of Salem belonged to the society, for they were mariners of long experience before they came ashore for good.

The East India Marine Society's chairman of entertainment well knew that staging a turtle feast was nothing to be attempted by amateurs. More than a hundred guests would be present; it had to be done the right way.

In the Salem of that time there were experts in a great many subjects. In architecture and carving beautiful things from wood it was Samuel McIntire. In building a ship Enos Briggs, Retire Becket or Ebenezer Mann had best be consulted. Certain merchants were well known for their almost documentary knowledge of conditions in such very different places as Naples, Quallah Battu, London, Calcutta, Kronstadt and Saint Kitts.

Anyone who wished to arm and fight a ship generally went to see Elias Hasket Derby, Jr., whose *Mount Vernon* had beaten enough enemies so that she was called "the little frigate." A person who had a document written in a strange foreign language was likely to get help from the Reverend William Bentley, minister of the East Church, and if it was the geography of hell that interested him, he could draw an excellent chart of the place after listening to the good parson's Sunday-morning sermon.

As for a turtle feast, there was one outstanding expert: Prince Hall. A tall, lean Negro of great dignity, he always carried himself with the air of one who ruled many. Indeed he did, for whenever a well-to-do person wished the best catering job in eastern Massachusetts, he sent word to Prince Hall in Boston, and when the time came he appeared with a dozen of his black men, or two dozen, if the banquet was a large one.

The host had no more worries, once Prince Hall had signified that he would take charge. Coming sometimes by vessel, sometimes by wagons loaded with his equipment, his utensils, and with his trusty Negroes perched on top of the load, he would arrive to direct the preparations. Every one of his men jumped when he gave an order; all arrangements were perfect, and the meal, when it reached the table, was always superb. Some who had seen him conduct his operations theorized that he was of royal African blood, descended from some kingly ancestor, or perhaps when an infant prince kidnapped by the black rascals who raided in the interior and sold their unhappy captives to the slave traders on the coast.

Whatever lines of distinguished ancestry there may have been no one ever could know, for Prince Hall never discussed the subject, probably for the excellent reason he himself did not know. But he was called "Prince" because of his bearing, his habit of command and his unusual capabilities. Deeply respected by all of African descent, he was master of the African Lodge of Masons in Boston, an organization which exists to this day, now bearing the title "Prince Hall Lodge."

Soon after the arrival of the turtle in Salem, the message from the East India Marine Society reached him and he summoned up his men and assembled his equipment. The brig *Cadet* of Salem lay at Long Wharf in Boston, discharging some of its Mediterranean cargo before sailing for her home port with the remainder. Hall engaged passage for himself and his men for the short twenty-mile trip to Salem. That same day the vessel made out past Boston Light, turned east past Nahant and Marblehead and then rounded Baker's Island, keeping Gale's Point, Manchester, to starboard. Under easy sail the brig followed down the Main Ship Channel, the heavily wooded Beverly shore to starboard, made a ninety-degree turn off Fort Pickering and, under double-reefed topsails, headed for her berth at Crowninshield's Wharf.

Prince Hall's first task, after he had visited the society's chairman of entertainment, was to see to the transportation of the West India turtle to Misery Island, where the feast was to be held. This time the creature rode in a ship's longboat, a much safer means of conveyance than the dugout canoe in which it had traveled from his sand bar on the island of Antigua. In the boat, and in another following it, were Hall's men, with the utensils and the tents to shelter them overnight on this harbor island.

With Prince Hall's arrival, the society's chairman was confident that all details were no more to be worried about. He turned to the matter of invitations, scribbling busily at his desk in his countinghouse on Derby Street, assisted by a couple of his clerks. Before sundown the clerks and some of his household servants were scurrying about town delivering the invitations. There was excitement in Salem that evening. A turtle feast catered by Prince Hall was always an event, and everyone of any note would be there.

When the huge flat box containing the turtle had been carried ashore at Misery Island, two miles out in Salem Bay and near the Beverly shore, Prince Hall gave the men a nod. They tipped the box and the turtle, after tedious weeks upside down, was again right side up. Hall took a bunch of parsley in one hand; in the other he held a cutlass.

He tossed the parsley to the ground before the monster. Swiftly the head darted from the shell, and the great beak snapped for the succulent greens. Even more swiftly Prince Hall swung the cutlass and flicked off the ugly head. It jumped forward a foot and lay on the grass, the parsley still in its jaws. The shining cutlass blade was buried deep in the sod.

The headless creature twitched in death spasms. Its blood spurted forth from the severed neck, some into a pan held by one of the men, more onto the sand and grass of the island. The men rigged a block and tackle and hoisted the body to a pole to drain, while Hall turned to give orders for collecting firewood, pitching the tents and making all secure for the night. Then, by the light of flickering torches, he directed the cutting up of carrots, peeling potatoes and the preparation of other vegetables for the morrow. On the island, as the torches burned low and the stars in their constellations told mariners that the night was no longer young, Hall ordered his men to quit.

They gathered around him, the master of their lodge, and for a moment there was complete silence except for the sound of little waves on the rocks and lapping on the beach of Misery Island. Then he led them in evening prayers, and after that they sang their evening hymn and the music of the two dozen Negro voices floated over the waters of the bay.

In the morning a gang of before-the-mast hands landed at the island, pitched the big tent and brought ashore the tables and chairs for the more than one hundred guests. From Salem came servants with boxes of silver, the blue and white Canton china plates and long white tablecloths. Prince Hall's men helped set the tables while others worked on the vegetables. In a fireplace of round beach stones a driftwood fire blazed. The great iron kettle was bubbling, and a Negro fed in more wood.

Over all this Prince Hall presided, deeply content. He had just finished the delicate task of removing the turtle's bottom shell and taking out the gall bladder. If in preparing a turtle the gall bladder broke, the flesh would be ruined by a taste strong enough to turn any human stomach. Prince Hall had removed the gall bladder successfully and tossed it into the fire, where it sizzled, smoked, popped and was gone.

By midmorning the guests began to set sail from the Salem water front. Trailing across Salem Bay all the way from Derby Wharf to Misery Island, scores of small craft—cutters and sloops and longboats—bore the members of the East India Marine Society and their guests to the turtle feast. One by one the small craft entered the cove on the island, and the blue-water mariners of Salem left their boats and climbed the sandy slope to watch the preparations for dinner and talk over matters that concerned their everyday affairs, from Napoleon's latest schemes to the best method of landing cargo through the surf of a beach in the South Pacific.

At last it was time to sit down, and they filed into the big tent to take their places at the tables. Then four of Prince Hall's Africans stepped smartly into the tent, bearing on their shoulders the great turtle shell. Now upside down, it contained a vast pie of Hall's making, steaming, topped with a delicately browned crust and garnished with wreaths of parsley and water cress. The enormous pie was designed to feed a hundred and it did, so well that few of the baked lobsters held in reserve ever came to the table.

Finally the great shell was empty, and the merchants and mariners of Salem were content. Then came the wine of Madeira, mellow yet potent. This wine was purchased at the Madeira Islands by Salem ships outward bound to India and stowed below, in the bilge, so that it might season during the long voyage to Calcutta or Bombay and return. This made it a wine of a greatly superior quality, advertised as "Madeira Twice Round the Cape," meaning it had gone around the Cape of Good Hope on both the outward-bound and homeward-bound voyages. Mellow indeed after a year in the hold, it was a drink for the quality.

The East India Marine Society, as they enjoyed their Madeira, drank toasts to all ships at sea, to the mariners who sailed them, to the women who waited for them. They drank to the success of American commerce, to the reverend clergy and to the eminent Reverend William Bentley, who was with them. Indeed, the scholarly parson was generally to be found wherever good food was being served.

Then they drank to the United States Navy and the gallant Commodore Preble and his Mediterranean squadron which was trying to teach the pirates of Tripoli that merchant vessels flying the American flag had best be let alone. Someone proposed a toast to the Bashaw of Tripoli; might he drag his anchor in a full gale, be blown onto a lee shore in hell and break up on Gehenna's rocks. Then it was bottoms up, with loud cheers.

William Gray, merchant of Salem, under whose house flag sailed thirty vessels, rose and held high his glass.

"To all our unfortunate countrymen who languish in the dungeons of Barbary," he proposed in a clear and ringing voice. "And may they have an early deliverance."

Applauding wildly and thumping the tables, the members rose, their glasses in their hands. This toast to the men of the merchant fleet held as slaves in the Barbary regencies and the crew of the United States frigate *Philadelphia,* now prisoners in Tripoli, was the high point of the turtle feast.

Late in the afternoon, when the dinner was at last over and the glow of the Madeira wine had subsided, the members of the Marine Society sailed back to Salem, their long line of small craft stringing out across the Middle Grounds from the Main Ship Channel to the wharves of the inner harbor. It was all over. The turtle, transported over a thousand miles, had come to the glorious end of his long career, and all Salem had enjoyed one of their famous get-togethers. At this banquet on Misery Island, while they ate or drank or waited, many a trade had been made, plenty of rum and pepper would change hands, guns would be purchased or swapped.

Sugar, coffee, indigo and tea would move from one warehouse to another or to the dockside to become part of an outward-bound cargo. Plans for new ships were thus begun, new voyages, new partners, and possibly a new turnpike or a new factory.

Still on Misery Island, Prince Hall and his men washed dishes, stowed their equipment, cleaned up and threw rubbish into the blazing fire. The Salem sailors struck the big tent and packed dishes to take back to town. Hall's men were not through until after sundown. Then they rested under the starlit sky, grateful for this time in which they might do nothing.

In the morning a sloop of the house of Forrester would call at the island to take them aboard for the return to Boston. Now they need to think only of their supper and to sit here awhile around the driftwood fire and sing some of the old songs until it was time for the evening prayer and another night in the little tents.

14 ᴜᴜᴏ

Life in the Old Navy

IT IS A LONG ROW of big thick books, a dozen of them. *Naval Documents* are the words on the backs of these books. *Operations, Barbary Wars* appears on some of them; *Quasi War with France* on others. This shelf full of volumes looks as if it awaits a professor with his green eyeshade and his note-book to sit down to paw over the pages and make occasional jottings.

Stay here long enough, and the old professor will doubt-less appear and go quietly to work. But if you decide to reach now for one of the books, blow the dust off the top and open it, you can begin to live life in the old navy back in those years between 1794 and 1805, for the men who wrote these logbooks and journals and letters and reports and orders were there. Thus you are there.

These men lived life in the old navy and they manned our ships. Long since have they sailed beyond the last horizon. But they wrote. We need only read what they wrote to live life in our navy in the days when the Republic was young.

Congress, by an Act of 1794, had provided for six frigates, fine ships that had few equals and no superiors in any navy of that day. After a ship was built, rigged and equipped, came the task of raising a crew, and this job had to be repeated with every new voyage of a ship, for the old crew would be paid off and go their ways. In 1803 at Boston, Captain Edward Preble was very busy indeed raising a crew for the frigate *Constitution*. He was ordered to sail his ship to the Mediterranean and join the squadron blockading Tripoli, but the frigate lay at Charlestown Navy Yard with no one aboard but a caretaker detail.

Recruiting was not easy, for those were days of great commercial prosperity, our merchant marine was flourishing and wages were high. Therefore the Secretary of the Navy told the navy agents in our various ports that they could advance a recruit two months' wages when he enlisted. The pay was ten dollars a month, so a man had twenty dollars in hand as soon as he signed.

Many a sailor used this to pay off debts ashore or to help provide for his family while he was at sea. A man of this sort could generally be counted on to be aboard when the ship sailed. However, another type of recruit took the twenty dollars to spend on a royal time along the water front. Such a man quite possibly would fail to remember so tiresome a detail as the frigate's date of departure. Some recruits, having taken the navy's money, then found a more attractive berth in a merchant ship and were far at sea by the time the frigate was ready to sail.

The navy took care of this problem very neatly. The recruit could have his twenty dollars, but he must have someone go bond for his appearance on the date of departure. Then if he did not report aboard, his surety was obliged to pay, and the navy was fully reimbursed for the amount it had given the man. Even so, the return of the money by the bondsman did not make up for the absence of that much-needed hand on the date of sailing.

Here and there in the naval records are oblique references to another old-fashioned method of filling up a crew. The Secretary of the Navy wrote to the agent that he could offer the landlords two dollars for each seaman. "The landlords can certainly procure men and failing in all other means, we must make it to their interest to exert themselves." The "landlords" referred to were the proprietors of the water-front rooming houses.

Their method was simple. If a sailor had been ashore long enough to use up his money, the landlord would put a pill known in modern colloquial speech as a "Mickey Finn" in the man's grog. This drug, a sleeping potion, would cause the sailor to become comatose. Then it was no trouble at all to put him aboard any vessel that needed him, and he would be in a deep sleep when the ship weighed anchor and put out to sea. As the man gradually came to, saw he was in a fore-castle and felt the long swell of the Atlantic beneath the vessel, he fully understood that he was setting forth upon a long voyage.

To this highhanded procedure was later applied the term "Shanghai," and the unsavory water-front characters who may be counted on for such recruiting methods are known as "crimps." It was effective, for when a ship was once at sea in the time before cable messages and radio, there was nothing a sailor could do but obey. A ship was its own little world; the captain was the emperor, and once a man was aboard, he did well not to think too much about the nature of his arrival.

Captain Preble needed four hundred men. It is not recorded how each one happened to become one of the crew of the *Constitution*. The captain sent Lieutenant Blake to New York to open a "rendezvous" and records in his journal on July 21, 1803, that the *Constitution* "cheered ship" in answer to the schooner *Sally*, which had come alongside with seventy men from New York. Three days later Midshipman Izard arrived from New York with fifty-six more men.

Captain Preble had sent Lieutenant Jenckes to Providence to recruit men, with the direction that he send them to Boston as soon as he should collect a "stage load." A stage full of mariners just signed on for a long cruise to the Mediterranean, the coach creaking along the Providence to Boston road, the men enjoying such refreshments as they may have purchased from the innkeeper before departure and becoming better acquainted with each other in the free and easy manner of shipmates, would be a subject to challenge the pen of any spinner of yarns of the olden times.

Earlier in July, Preble had noted in his journal that England had declared war on France. This, he observed, "increases our success in recruiting foreign seamen, as they dare not trust to the protection the merchant service affords them and are sure of being safe from impressment with us." This remark, of course, referred to British seafaring men. In time of war Britain's Royal Navy, hungry for men, used to examine every merchant vessel, no matter what its nationality, to see if any Englishmen were serving aboard. If so, they were promptly seized and put to work in the British navy.

Many an American, unjustly impressed on the feeble pretext he was English, was forced to do long service in the Royal Navy. Although such injustices occurred with frequency and were so often repeated as to become one of the causes of the

War of 1812, it is nevertheless true that many Englishmen actually were in the American merchant marine and the United States Navy.

Even though the *Constitution*'s muster roll grew with local recruitment and the arrivals from New York and Providence, Captain Preble was not pleased. "The men we have engaged here are not such as I wish. Wages in the merchant service are so high that the best men will not ship with us. I do not believe I have twenty native Americans on board."

Preble sailed with this crew that did not satisfy him. When he reached Gibraltar, he managed to sign aboard some Italians. At Valletta twenty Maltese joined them. Later, when a Tripoline vessel was captured, seven Greeks, slaves of the Bashaw, were found aboard. They at once volunteered and forthwith became members of the *Constitution*'s complement.

The variety of nationalities represented in the frigate's crew may startle those who think of the early navy as being manned by native Americans, by which they generally mean descendants of those who came over on the *Mayflower*. Since Britishers did not dare to serve in the American merchant marine, but did serve in the American navy because there they were safe from impressment, it is quite possible many of the *Constitution*'s crew were British. True, they were not native Americans, but it would seem that they were nearly enough so to have satisfied Preble. Professor Samuel Eliot Morison has stated that the old-time Yankees were only two-thirds Anglo-Saxon stock and the other third was Irish, Scotch and French. Thus many in the *Constitution*'s crew, although not native, may have been in the process of becoming so.

Preble left Boston with his crew of "foreigners" and added Italians and Greeks, all of whom served under him for over a year. What were these men at the end of the year? Many would be ready to say that they were then Yankees of the first water. If a group of men serving for one year in the frigate *Constitution* with Captain Edward Preble as a teacher did not become good Yankees by the end of that time, it would be astonishing.

"When do we eat?" has always been one of the great questions with hard-working men everywhere. The Congress of the United States intended that the United States Navy should have a name for well-fed crews. So this would not depend on the whims of various commanding officers, Congress passed an act setting forth exactly what food a sailor in the navy was entitled to every day in the week. The list as it appears in the statute is as follows:

Sunday: 1 lb. of bread, 1½ lbs of beef, ½ pint of rice. (The bread was not what we get today from the baker; it was a sort of hardtack or ship's biscuit. The beef was salt beef, taken out of a cask by the cook, soaked overnight and cooked on the galley stoves.)

Monday: 1 lb. of bread, 1 lb. of pork, ½ pint of peas or beans, 4 ounces of cheese. (The pork was salt pork from barrels.)

Tuesday: 1 lb. of bread, 1½ lbs. of beef, 1 lb. of potatoes or turnips, pudding. (The pudding was a luxury and was probably the famous "plum duff.")

Wednesday: 1 lb. of bread, 2 ounces of butter or in lieu thereof 6 ounces of molasses, 4 ounces of cheese, ½ pint of rice. (The butter and the cheese were a real effort to give navy men something good in the way of rations and were doubtless very heartening if unspoiled.)

Thursday: 1 lb. of bread, 1 lb. of pork, ½ pint of peas or beans. (This is a day when Jack Tar would have to live on the memories of better days.)

Friday: 1 lb. of bread, 1 lb. of salf fish, 2 ounces of butter or a gill of oil and 1 lb. of potatoes. (This provided some variety. The butter or oil would help make the "bread" a less dry and uninteresting ration.)

Saturday: 1 lb. of bread, 1 lb. of pork, ½ pint of beans and 4 ounces of cheese. (The cheese was all the sailors got as an extra on the weekend.)

The Act of Congress went on to order that each man should have a half pint of distilled spirits per day or a quart of beer. This was a feature the old navy provided its men that we do not have in our time. There was real necessity for this half pint of spirits, generally rum, which is not understood until we pause to examine working conditions aboard the vessels of the old sailing navy.

A ship could not be navigated unless a large number of men worked in the open, exposed to the weather, to make and take in sail. Today the vessel is operated by the efforts of men in engine room and fireroom, entirely sheltered. The old-time sailor, when he came off watch cold and sometimes soaking wet, could not go to a forecastle with steam heat and strip off his clothing. The old-time forecastle had no heat. The best he could do was get the wet clothes off and climb into his bunk or hammock, so cold his teeth were chattering. That is where the distilled-spirits ration was of tremendous value. With a cup of rum to pour into his cold interior, most chills vanished.

Today we think of rum or any hard liquor as a vice if indulged in habitually. In those days when the science of heating as we know it was practically unheard of, rum was a health measure, plain and simple. The navy did not issue rum so that the men could make merry, but rather to keep the men well. Occasionally some sailor by ingenuity managed to save each day's allowance in a receptacle hidden somewhere aboard ship until he had a quart or more. Then, possessed of this generous supply, he would put in a day doing some really serious drinking. Problems of keeping warm would vanish; so also would all burdens of duty and responsibility. No longer would he have any superiors aboard ship; any petty officer or, for that matter, a commissioned officer who presumed to criticize him he would insult, and perhaps he would administer corporal punishment to some offensive person by punching him in the nose.

The treatment for these cases was routine. In the firm grasp of however many shipmates as were necessary to hold him, he was hauled before the captain, the evidence was heard, and sentence was pronounced.

"A dozen," the captain would say.

Off came the culprit's shirt. He was triced up, a boatswain's mate swung the rope, the man howled with each wallop, and when it was over a bucket of cold sea water was thrown upon his welted back. Then the boastwain gave him a heavy kick in the stern transom and ordered him back to duty. Generally by the end of the procedure the man was completely sober, all liquor-induced fancies of superiority had fled, he realized he was only a seaman in the navy and he obeyed orders without question.

Everything in the list of navy rations provided by the Act of Congress could be stored for a long voyage. The pork and beef were salt provisions, put up in casks and preserved in brine until ready for use. This required casks that were a good job of cooperage, for should the brine or "pickle" leak out, the meat would spoil and have to be hove overboard. The name of the supplier was on each cask so that if the meat was inedible a report could be made and the navy would claim a refund.

These salt meats had to be taken from the cask the day before use and put to soak overnight to get some of the salt out before cooking. An oaken tub with brass hoops was used for this overnight soaking. Aboard the *Constitution* today this tub may be viewed, its oak varnished and its brass hoops well shined.

This tub was invariably called the "harness cask" for an excellent reason. Any real deep-water mariner would swear that the salt beef issued the sailors was not beef at all but actually the flesh of old horses who had outlived their working days and were no longer fit for anything but ship's provisions. Therefore the tub in which the old horses were soaked was the "harness cask," and this conviction is expressed in the old rhyme, recited with a little drama by the sailors who were rendering this classic. One would pick up a piece of "salt hoss," look at it and address it thus:

> Old Hoss, Old Hoss, what brought you here,
> From Sacarap to Portland Pier?

Thereupon another sailor, speaking for the old horse, would chime in:

> I've carted stone this many a year,
> Till killed by blows and sore abuse,
> They salted me down for sailor's use.
> The sailors they do me despise,
> They turn me over and damn my eyes,
> Cut off my meat and scrape my bones,
> And pitch me over to Davy Jones.

The recital generally ended with the piece of "salt hoss" being flung over the lee rail. The character "Davy Jones," above referred to, was the proprietor of the famous "Davy Jones Locker," the sailor's term for the bottom of the sea.

One glance at the list of rations in the Act of Congress shows how lacking it is in any vitamin-bearing fresh foods. This is a diet planned for two main purposes: high energy content for hard-working men and suitability for storage for the duration of a long voyage. As a result there were many cases of scurvy aboard the old sailing ships, a disease directly resulting from dietary deficiencies. It was known that lack of fresh provisions was the cause of this disease that disabled so many mariners.

Whenever a ship called at any port, the captain's first concern was to obtain water; his second, firewood for the galley stoves. Then, with these two absolute essentials taken care of, the captain turned his attention to getting all the fresh provisions possible. The value of fresh foods was beginning to be understood in the early days of the navy, although the word "vitamin" was not to appear for more than a century. A few incidents show the efforts of commanding officers to overcome the deficiencies of the salt beef and hard tack rations.

In 1802 Captain Alexander Murray wrote the Secretary of the Navy: "Potatoes and onions as well as every other kind of vegetable ought to be allowed whenever they can be procured as very contributory to the health of the crew." From the tone of this statement, Captain Murray seems to feel he is setting forth a truth not generally understood. Naval regulations required that every ship be provided with a seine so that when possible a netting party might be sent out to obtain fresh fish for the crew.

While the *Constitution* was in Algiers Bay in November 1803, the ship's surgeon told Captain Preble that fresh meat and vegetables were much needed for the use of the sick and to preserve the health of those who were well. Plainly the surgeon had a number of scurvy cases in the sick bay and feared there would soon be more. Preble thereupon procured from ashore fifty bushels of potatoes, fifty bushels of onions, four hundred head of cabbage, a thousand lemons and oranges, six dozen fowl and four bushels of barley. Again, at Syracuse, fresh mutton and fresh vegetables were obtained for the ship's company, and upon other occasions poultry and fruit were purchased there. When the Mediterranean squadron called at Tunis, the navy bought five bullocks, thirty dozen fowl, four dozen pigeons, thirty sheep, a thousand eggs, cabbages, oranges and lemons. A supply of corn was obtained to feed the livestock, which were kept in pens on deck until ready for slaughter.

The idea of pens of animals and coops of poultry on the deck of a man-of-war is doubtless shocking to a modern navy man. In the old navy the decks were scrubbed daily with "holy-stones" until they were spotless, yet the captain was willing to accept the ordure and disorder of animal pens, straw and hay if thereby he could have fresh food for his men and avoid attacks of the dreaded scurvy. If an enemy ship hove in sight, the command "Clear for Action" really meant something, for then the pens, the animals and the hay went overboard so the guns could be used without any impediment whatsoever.

The best account of scurvy and its cure appears in that great classic of the sea, Dana's *Two Years before the Mast*. The *Alert* had left the California coast with its cargo of hides and had sailed down the entire coast of South America, around

Cape Horn and had come north to the latitude of the West Indies when scurvy began to appear among these men so long a time without fresh food.

Of one victim Dana says: "His legs swelled, he could not walk, his flesh lost its elasticity so that if pressed it would not return to its shape, and his gums swelled so that he could not open his mouth. His breath became very offensive, he lost all strength and spirit, he could eat nothing and unless something was done for him, he would be a dead man in a week at the rate at which he was sinking." Here is a description of a patient's symptoms comprehensive enough to satisfy a professor in a medical school.

At this juncture, with such a very ill man lying helpless in his bunk, the *Alert* spoke an American ship bound for Curaçao with provisions and was able to buy half a boatload of new potatoes and onions. The cook took the potatoes raw, pounded them in a mortar and gave the potato juice to the sick man to drink, a teaspoonful at a time. He rinsed it about his gums and throat. At first this produced a shuddering through his whole frame, then acute pain all over his body, but he drank a spoonful every hour and soon he was able to walk and eat.

So rapid was this sailor's recovery, writes Dana, that in ten days he was at the masthead, furling a royal. The other sailors ate the onions raw at every meal by the dozen and filled their pockets with them to eat during their watch on deck. Their bodies were starved for vitamins, and the onions satisfied their craving.

The problem of scurvy aboard ships long at sea was finally solved by a British doctor whose experiments conclusively proved that it is a disease of vitamin deficiency. It was found that the best preventive is lime juice, which is easily stored for long periods of time. Then the British Parliament passed a law requiring that lime juice be issued to the crew on all English ships. Other nations followed the lead of the English, and thus ended this great scourge of the sea. Thenceforth sailors referred to every British ship as a "lime juicer" and, in America, at least, any Englishman was known as a "limey."

It is, of course, true that no navy can be run without discipline, any more than can an army. To take the ragtag and bobtail of the water front, men shanghaied from rooming houses, farm boys, foreigners and the ordinary run of landsmen and fashion them into a navy required strong discipline. The officers of the small American navy were equal to the task.

Captain Preble, when he commanded the *Constitution,* was an example of a commander who ran a taut ship. Negligence in the performance of duty earned a seaman twelve lashes; so did drunkenness. Stealing from the ship's stores was good for thirty-six lashes.

One day Preble went ashore at the American naval base at Syracuse on the island of Sicily to inspect the repair work being done on Lieutenant Stephen Decatur's schooner *Enterprise.* During our war with Tripoli the governor of Syracuse had gladly given the American squadron the use of his harbor as a base, because this meant Sicily would be free of raids by the Barbary pirates as long as the Americans stayed. All four Barbary regencies had frequently raided in these waters and had even landed, looted towns and carried off dozens of Sicilians to be held in slavery in North Africa until they were ransomed. No Barbary pirate vessel dared come anywhere near waters in which an American man-of-war might be, so the governor of Syracuse had a bargain. Upon arrival with the *Constitution,* Preble had taken command of the squadron with the rank of commodore.

When, on this particular day, the commodore reached the men working ashore on the repair of the schooner's rigging, he discovered they had acquired a quantity of Italian red wine to lighten their labors. The wine had done its work well, and the men were in so uplifted a state that the presence of the commodore himself awed them not at all.

Apparently the men treated Preble quite unceremoniously, for as soon as he returned to his flagship, he wrote Decatur as follows: "Sir; Your men on shore for the purpose of fitting your rigging were this afternoon most of them drunk. One of your men is in irons on board this ship for impertinence to me." Preble went on to order Decatur to make an inquiry. It is easy to imagine the mortification a junior officer must have felt upon learning that his men had behaved so badly in the presence of the commodore of the squadron that it had been necessary to put one of them in irons.

Inefficiency brought quick punishment. The acting boat-swain and the gunner were discharged from their positions and sent to do duty before the mast. In today's parlance they were "broken" or "busted." Another petty officer, a ship's corporal, got thirty-six lashes for attempting to fumigate part of the ship without orders, for neglect of duty and for permitting the rope yarns used for fumigating to break into a blaze. This man had exposed the ship to the danger of fire and the penalty was severe.

Captain Bainbridge, captain of the frigate *Essex* in 1801, promulgated these rules, among others, for the government of his ship:

1. Should any person quit his station before he is regularly

relieved or ordered to do so, he is to ride the spanker boom for three hours the succeeding watch and his grog stopped for three days successively.

2. For a second offense of similar nature, he is to be put in irons and flogged as I may direct and lose his grog for fifteen days.

The spanker boom projects from the base of the mizzenmast over the quarter-deck and out over the taffrail. If the spanker sail was set, it is hard to see how the culprit could be made to ride the boom unless he were perched on the very end. In that case he would be sitting out over the water astern or off the ship's quarter, and when the frigate came about on the opposite tack, the boom would whip from one side to the other and the man astride the end of it would do well if he stayed aboard.

One might wonder whether Bainbridge's punishment for the first offense is not more severe than that for the second. However, the second offender was not only flogged but deprived of his grog for fifteen days. Parching the insides of a man accustomed to enjoying a half pint of rum as part of his daily diet may have been the cruelest penalty of all. This punishment seems harsh, yet it is to be remembered there are few offenses in naval or military life more serious than leaving one's post of duty. It could result in the loss of the ship and the lives of many of the crew.

The navy had forms to be filled out even in the earliest days. We have a form for the daily report of prisoners which was filled out aboard the *Constitution* on February 12, 1804, in this way:

NAMES	QUALITY	BY WHOM CONFINED	WHEN	HOW	CRIME
J. Cross	Seamen	Lt. Dent	Jan. 25	In irons	Drunkenness.

This man must have behaved outrageously to be kept in irons eighteen days for drunkenness. It does not appear what he said or did to Lieutenant Dent to warrant this punishment.

The other form we have is the "Women's List," kept by the master-at-arms to record the behavior of female visitors aboard while the ship was in port. Unfortunately the blank preserved in the naval records is not filled out. It is set up as follows:

WOMEN'S NAMES	WITH WHOM	MARRIED OR SINGLE	WHEN RECEIVED ON BOARD	CONDUCT

Sometimes it was necessary to deal with a really difficult prisoner. It is recorded in the sailing master's journal of one such that he was "a notorious character and was received last Sunday from the U.S. brig *Argus* in irons." He was charged with refusing duty, contempt of a commissioned officer, insolence to a non-commissioned officer and attempting to desert. Apparently the captain of the *Argus* thought this was so serious it should be dealt with by the commodore himself. The commodore dealt with him; the sentence was forty-eight lashes.

Another disciplinary problem was desertion. Of course, it is expected that there will be an occasional man who wanders off while on shore leave, because he is tired of shipboard routine or sees an opportunity for a good berth on a merchant vessel. In the old days such deserters were called "run men."

It may come as a surprise to many to learn that the real desertion problem was with men who slipped away to join Britain's Royal Navy. Stories of the hard and cruel life in the English navy of that day, told by Americans impressed into service, make it difficult to believe any man in his right mind would join it voluntarily. Yet while the American squadron lay at Gibraltar during our war with Tripoli, men deserted both the *Constitution* and the *Siren* to join the British. This they did by slipping over the side at night and swimming to the English vessels, where they were well received and at once enlisted. Midshipman Henry Wadsworth's diary states that at Gibraltar the British anchored near the American men-of-war "in order to give our men an opportunity of swimming on board of them," and Preble wrote to the Secretary of the Navy that "everyone who receives punishment for crimes deserts if opportunity offers." After reading of the punishments Preble meted out in his determination to have a "taut ship," one may see how a sailor aboard the *Constitution* might have wondered if life in the Royal Navy would be better.

There was an exchange of acrimonious notes between various American commanders and their British counterparts. Captain Gore of the Royal Navy wrote to Preble that the deserters he had received were actually Englishmen, as were many sailors in the American navy. "Finding that their Sovereign is engaged in a serious war with an inveterate foe," wrote Captain Gore, "they wish to return to their own flag, but are detained by force."

The inveterate foe was, of course, Napoleon. Anyone reading what was written by Englishmen during the time of the Napoleonic Wars can readily see that they hated him at least as thoroughly as their descendants ever hated Adolf Hitler. Therefore it is quite possible some of the deserters were Englishmen who felt a strong call to help the mother country in its bitter wars with the "Corsican upstart," as the British liked to term the Emperor of France.

Relations between the British and American navies were generally good during our war with Tripoli. The facilities of the British bases at Gibraltar and Malta were offered our squadron, and supplies were made available. The matter of deserters was the one difficulty between the two navies. Preble wrote to the Secretary of the Navy on October 23, 1803: "At Malta our ships lay so near the shore that it will be impossible to prevent desertion, which has determined me to make Syracuse the deposit of all our provisions and stores and the general rendezvous of our squadron."

When any American man-of-war did have occasion to call at Malta, the commander ordered out a guard boat to patrol all night to prevent sailors from deserting by swimming ashore. However, the passage of nine years was to make a tremendous difference. The English, with a disregard for American feelings that is astonishing, continued a policy of impressing sailors from our merchantmen. This practice became general, and British officers took any likely looking mariner who spoke English, inventing cynical and outrageous lies as to their nationality.

So by 1812 the relations between the two nations had worsened until there was bitter hostility. No longer did American commanders have to worry about any sailor deserting the ship to sign on with the Royal Navy. And when war broke in 1812 it was not necessary to recruit crews the hard way, as did Preble in 1803. Men pressed forward to volunteer. One is reminded of a similar situation a great many years later when the navy recruiting officer in Boston went to his office in the Federal Building on Monday, December 8, 1941, and had difficulty getting out at his floor because the corridor was packed with young men eager to enlist, following the news of the attack on Pearl Harbor.

In the War of 1812 the captain of the *Constitution* would

have had no occasion to say, as did Preble in 1803, that he did not think there were more than twenty native Americans in the crew. In the frigate's crew in that war there were eighty men from one town, that most nautical of American communities, Marblehead. When the two British frigates pursued the *Constitution* toward Marblehead and the captain sent word forward to see if any man in the crew knew those waters well enough to guide the ship into the harbor, he was a bit taken aback when fourscore men presented themselves on the quarter-deck. Samuel Green was selected to take the wheel and, with the freely offered advice of seventy-nine of his fellow townsmen, he brought the frigate into Marblehead harbor.

In the old navy every effort was made to preserve the health of the men. A frigate was provided with a surgeon and two surgeon's mates. In battle they occupied the cockpit, which was in the hold, out of reach of cannon balls and flying splinters. Most of the surgeon's work was in treating the sick, a day-to-day, never-ending chore in a group the size of a frigate's crew.

The surgeon was a man of some medical knowledge, so the crew received better care than in the merchant service, where the captain was ship's doctor, as well as ship's clergyman. A merchant captain usually provided himself with a Symptom Book, which gave descriptions of the various ailments to which the human body is subject. A chest of medicines with each bottle numbered came with the Symptom Book, and at the end of each description of a particular disease in the text was given the number of the bottle in the chest from which pills should be given to the patient.

This system worked better on some occasions than others. One sea captain, after reading the Symptom Book, made up his mind what the sailor's illness was and noted that this called for a pill from bottle Number 8. It turned out that bottle Number 8 was empty. This did not trouble the captain. He was aware that four plus four equals eight and always has, so he gave the sailor two pills from Number 4. The patient became much worse but managed to survive, doubtless due to rum administered by the boatswain and an emetic compounded by the ship's cook.

From this experience the captain learned that in the field of medicine this sort of mathematical logic cannot be depended on. In the Symptom Book were directions for setting broken bones and this also the captain had to do, with two men sitting on the patient to hold him still, another administering rum and the mate reading each step in the procedure as the captain followed the instructions. Navy men were more fortunate; they had a surgeon who had done the various procedures before, or at least said he had. Aboard the *Constitution* today, at Charlestown Navy Yard, may be seen the lancets, tweezers and bullet probes from the old-time surgeon's instrument case.

Of life on shipboard we have only a slight glimpse now and then. An officer was not allowed to live on a plane above the men so far as food was concerned. One of Preble's rules was that choice pieces of beef were never to be selected purposely for the officers, nor were the officers to select casks of the best wine or spirits for their own use. Thus did the commodore try to keep his officers mindful of the welfare of the men, a principle which is respected today in the American naval and military services.

Shore leave was valued then, as now. No man was allowed to bring liquor on board, and any found in boats bringing back a liberty party was promptly hove overboard. A letter written in December 1802 aboard the frigate *Adams* in Gibraltar Bay describes a man just returned from shore leave: "O'Bannon is one of the happiest fellows living. He has just returned from spending the evening with a brilliant circle of Spanish ladies and by way of consolation for the loss of their company, philosophy and the fiddle is called to his aid. On the latter he is now playing 'Hogs in the Cornfield.' "

This is the same O'Bannon, a marine, who was later to distinguish himself in General Eaton's gallant expedition to capture Derna on the shores of Tripoli. Commodore Preble in November of 1803 wrote to the Secretary of the Navy: "I have on board the *Constitution* many remarkably fine young men whose conduct promises great things to their country."

It is interesting to observe that Preble was becoming a little happier about his personnel. And what he wrote to the Secretary turned out to be true. The young men on his ship and in his squadron lived and fought under his strict command; they received much schooling from his exacting leadership and later they were referred to as "Preble's Boys." These young officers rose in rank and in 1812, when war with England broke out, they were the heart of the officer corps of the navy. Of the long list of officers who distinguished themselves in the War of 1812 a large proportion were those who learned so much from the stern rule of Commodore Edward Preble, and their names have lived in American naval history.

15

The Essex Frigate

IN THE EARLY DAYS of the Republic the Third Congress, by the statute of March 27, 1794, authorized our first naval building program. The statute, entitled "An Act to Provide a Naval Armament," began with these words: "Whereas the depredations committed by the Algerine corsairs on the commerce of the United States render it necessary that a naval force be provided for its protection . . ." At that time the "Algerines" were annoying American commerce more than the other three regencies of the Barbary Coast of North Africa, although later these others, Morocco, Tunis and Tripoli, did a great deal of damage to our merchant shipping.

In 1794 the Turkish Empire reached all the way to the Atlantic Ocean. The conquering Turks held Greece, the Balkans and the entire Middle East as well. To govern these distant lands, the Sultan allowed a local ruler to exercise almost complete sovereignty and do as he pleased as long as he paid an annual tribute at Constantinople. Each of these potentates of the Barbary regencies, variously called the Bey or Dey or Bashaw, had his own navy—ships called "corsairs," which were in reality engaged in organized piracy.

They seized the ships of any weak nation, appropriated the vessels and cargoes, held the crew until ransom was paid, and if ransom was not provided for a man, he was cast into slavery to do hard labor until he died. The United States was one of the weak nations. Its commerce was active and it had no navy. It was a country that desired only peace and the opportunity to work hard. The 1794 statute is a landmark in American history, for it was the beginning of the United States Navy. No longer were the Turkish robbers of the Barbary Coast to be allowed to consider the United States a defenseless nation.

Fortune smiled on this new navy at the outset in the selection of Joshua Humphreys as designer of the vessels. With unusual judgment he drew plans for six frigates that would never have to fear battle with any other frigate afloat. *Constitution, President, United States, Constellation, Congress* and *Chesapeake*—these names have come down through the years since 1794 with the ring of immortality. Never did a navy start with better ships. Of these, three were to leave paths of glory in the history of their country, one was a hard-luck ship who did her duty, one was a work horse who did not happen upon great moments and one had a tragic career. Two of them are afloat today, carefully preserved by a nation that wishes to remember their achievements in making the world realize that here was not a weak power to be insulted at will.

Five more frigates were to follow, planned in 1798 when the growing belligerence of France resulted in ever-mounting attacks by her men-of-war and privateers on the American merchant marine. The government did not have the money for this second naval building program, even though French depredations made it urgently necessary, so the Act of Con-

gress provided that public subscriptions would be accepted
and interest-bearing "stock" would be issued to all who con-
tributed money to construct these men-of-war.

Along the coast merchants who had interests in the profitable foreign trade came forward with subscriptions in varying
amounts. The money was raised, and the keels were laid down.
The frigates *Philadelphia, New York* and *Boston* were built
in the cities for which they were named; the *John Adams* was
built in Charleston, South Carolina, and the *Essex* in Salem,
Massachusetts. Three of these were vessels that did their work
but never came to greatness. One of them, the *Philadelphia,*
had hard luck and yet her end came gloriously. The smallest
of the frigates, the *Essex,* a thirty-two-gun ship built on Winter Island in Salem harbor, made for herself one of the most
unusual careers of any man-of-war that ever flew the American flag.

One hundred of the Salem people subscribed $74,700 to
the building of this man-of-war. Some came forward with
sums as small as ten or twenty-five dollars, but most were sub-
stantial. Topping the list with ten thousand dollars each were
Billy Gray and King Derby, the town's two greatest merchants, men whose vessels might be seen in New York or
Philadelphia, London or Naples, possibly waiting a wind
favorable to a passage up the Hooghly River to Calcutta, or
trading among the islands of the South Sea. Salem knew its
trade would perish if its ships could not sail the seven seas unmolested.

The attitude of the people of Salem in 1798 is best seen in
an advertisement inserted in one of the newspapers by Enos
Briggs, builder of the frigate *Essex:* "True lovers of liberty
and of your country, step forth and give your assistance in

building the frigate to oppose French insolence and piracy."

The builder then went on to ask that the people of Essex County offer to sell him white oak timber: "Let every man in possession of a white oak tree feel ambitious to be foremost in hurrying the timber down to Salem to fill the complement wanting where the noble structure is to be fabricated to maintain your sights upon the Seas. Your largest and longest trees are wanted and the arms of them for knees and rising timber. Four trees are wanted for the keel, which altogether will measure 146 feet in length and hew 16 inches square."

The subscribers to the fund to build the ship held a meeting in Salem on October 25, 1798, and voted to construct a frigate of thirty-two guns, which they decided to name for their beloved Essex County. The meeting named Colonel Hackett of Portsmouth, New Hampshire, to prepare the model and superintend construction. Enos Briggs, who had built fifty merchant vessels in Salem, was given the contract to construct the frigate, and on the committee elected by the subscribers to carry their votes into effect were William Gray, John Norris and Jacob Ashton, Esquires, and Captain Benjamin Hodges and Captain Ichabod Nichols. The first three designated as "Esquires" were leading merchants, and those who were named as "Captain" were shipmasters. The title "Captain" was not used loosely in maritime Salem.

It is interesting to note that the United States Government was not consulted in the execution of this project. Salem men raised the money and Salem men thereupon proceeded to design, build and name this man-of-war without feeling it at all necessary to bother the government authorities in charge of the navy.

Parson Bentley, who observed everything that went on and recorded it in his famous diary, noted on January 5, 1799, that timber for the frigate "comes in merrily," and on January 8 he reported that it was unusually good sledding for bringing in timber for the ship. Briggs reached deep into Essex County for his white oak; in the forests of Danvers, Topsfield, Boxford and Andover the men were in the woods, axes were ringing and great trees came crashing to the ground as the people responded to the challenge to build a ship that would show the French that Yankee mariners were to sail the oceans of the world in complete freedom.

The keel was laid in April and thereafter, with plenty of oak logs sledded in during the winter, the work at the site on Salem Neck went forward at a great pace. Chips flew as the men with ship adzes hewed out the timbers; the hammers rang as the ribs and planks were spiked into place; smoke rose from the forges of the blacksmiths and the fires of the coppersmiths.

How a ship the equivalent of a modern light cruiser was built for about $75,000 may be somewhat understood when the pay scales of the workmen in 1799 are examined. Laborers received $1 a day, joiners $1.25 a day and carpenters $1.50. Timber was not brought from far places; it was cut in the nearby towns and then hauled to the shipyard by the oxen and horses of the local people without freight charges.

By August the cannon for the frigate had arrived, long twelve-pounders not as powerful as the eighteen- and twenty-four-pounders of the larger frigates, yet an armament very effective indeed if served by good gunners. Had these long guns remained with the frigate, one page of our history would have read differently.

Late in September the cables, done in the Briggs ropewalk at Salem, were ready to be taken down to the frigate. Their delivery is evidence of what this ship meant to the town. These enormous lines were picked up by two hundred men and boys, who lifted them to their shoulders. Then, preceded by a fife and drum, the cables were carried down to the place where the *Essex* lay on the stocks of the shipyard, with martial music to keep everyone in step.

September 30, 1799, was launching day. On Winter Island (now called Salem Willows) twelve thousand people were gathered. Seats near the ship sold for twenty-five cents each, and the adjacent shore line was covered with people. In nearby Beverly and on Marblehead's bold Naugus Head crowds awaited the moment when the *Essex* would first feel the tremor of life along her keel.

The ways were greased with tallow and men with mauls knocked away the blocks and wedges. At last the frigate moved. A bottle was smashed over her bow, and down the ways she went, as the tallow with which they were lubricated smoked from the heat generated by the friction of her movement. With an epic splash the *Essex* entered the waters of Salem harbor, floating jauntily and gracefully in her element. Great cheers rolled over the bay, and the frigate's battery of twelve-pounders, mounted on shore, thundered a salute to the new man-of-war.

"She moved easily and the launch was happy," wrote the Reverend Bentley in his diary. "No accident interrupted the Joy of the day." This was important, for the events of launching day are considered omens of the future history of a ship, and anything which goes wrong may cast a shadow over a vessel, for mariners are the most superstitious of people.

By December of 1799 the *Essex* was ready for sea, guns in place, ballast below, provisions and stores aboard, and a crew signed on with Captain Edward Preble in command. He had twenty-six twelve-pounders on the gun deck and ten six-pounders on the quarter-deck. Preble wrote that he wanted nine-pounders instead of sixes, but he had to sail with what he had. On December 22 the frigate left Salem for Newport, there to join the frigate *Congress* and escort a convoy of merchant vessels bound for Batavia on the island of Java.

Trouble for the convoy, which sailed January 6, 1800, soon arrived. The rigging of the *Congress* was set up in cold weather, with the result that it went slack as the ships sailed south into warm latitudes. The masts of a ship are supported by the shrouds, which are stout ropes running from the sides of the vessel, and by forestays and backstays. When a gale came up, the captain of the *Congress* was either unaware that his standing rigging was slack or he failed to get his men to the task of making it taut in time. Consequently the blow dismasted the vessel so that she was a drifting hulk, helpless until her crew managed to rig jury masts with which she could limp back to the United States.

No such mishap befell the *Essex,* a circumstance which those familiar with our naval history of the era will be ready to ascribe to the fact that Edward Preble was in command. Not in our entire history have we had a more competent officer, so we may assume he had his rigging taut well before the arrival of the gale.

Thus the frigate *Essex* sailed on toward the Indies, guarding the convoy all alone and well able to do so. Rounding the Cape of Good Hope, the southernmost tip of Africa, she was the first American man-of-war to fly the national colors in those eastern seas. On this her maiden voyage she proved to be a smart craft and a fast sailer. The French men-of-war and privateers, seeing that the merchantmen were convoyed by this capable-appearing frigate, minded their own business.

At Batavia, the chief port of Java, the *Essex* saluted the Dutch flag with sixteen guns. Before paying this public courtesy to the flag of another nation, Captain Preble first had a talk with the Dutch commander to make sure that he would return the compliment with a sixteen-gun salute to the American colors. Preble was no one to leave anything to chance.

Returning from Batavia with fourteen American vessels in the convoy, the *Essex* encountered an American ship which had been captured by a French privateer, now manned by Frenchmen with the Yankee crew in irons below. This situation Preble and his men speedily reversed.

The next event in the career of the *Essex* was service in our war with Tripoli, which commenced in 1801. With the *President, Philadelphia* and *Enterprise* she formed the first American Mediterranean squadron. Her work was routine, helping with the blockade and assuring the other Barbary Powers by her presence off their shores that it would be un-rewarding to intervene in this war.

It is impossible ever to foretell whether great moments will come to a man-of-war. The names *Enterprise, Intrepid, Philadelphia, Constitution, Argus* and *Syren* are remembered in the history of the conflict with Tripoli; the others did their duty without unusual incident. This war ended, but days of action for the *Essex* lay some years ahead.

As time passed, relations between the United States and Britain, who was engaged in the deadly struggle against Na-

poleon, grew steadily worse. Determined to strangle the
French Empire economically, the British interfered with
American commerce whenever bound to or from a French-
held port. The result was heavy losses for the French and
for the American merchants as well. Even worse was the
British policy of searching American ships under pretext
of looking for Englishmen serving in the American crews.
So enormous was the British navy at this time that they
were always short of seamen. Therefore the test of English
nationality was likely to be whether the sailor spoke English.

The bitterness created by the impressment of thousands
of American sailors to endure the hell of life in the British
navy at last built up to the point where war was declared. To
the tiny American navy was handed the assignment of con-
ducting aggressive operations against Britain's navy of one
thousand warships and against her merchant marine, much
of it consisting of armed vessels. The *Essex,* commanded by
another of the outstanding captains whom America was fortunate enough to have in those days, departed on July 8, 1812,
to cruise against the British.

Captain David Porter and his frigate gathered in nine
British merchant vessels as prizes. He recaptured five American privateers and merchantmen which had been taken by
the British navy and with prize crews were headed for some
English port.

Then one night he came up with a British convoy that
was transporting a thousand soldiers from Barbados to Quebec. With the *Essex* disguised as a merchant vessel, he drew
alongside the last ship in the convoy, spoke her, talked to
her master and learned the facts about the convoy. Porter
ordered his frigate to draw ahead until she came up with

the next vessel in the convoy. This Britisher became alarmed, but before he could give a signal, up came the gun ports of the *Essex,* and twenty guns were rolled out to calm this excited shipmaster. He was ordered to follow the *Essex* or be blown out of the water. He followed.

After taking the British vessel out of the convoy, she was examined and found to have 197 English soldiers aboard. Placing a guard aboard, Captain Porter at once took his frigate back into the convoy to cut out another ship. But daybreak was too near; the English in the gray light of dawn discovered that an American warship was in the convoy with them.

Falling back, the *Essex* now dropped her disguise and the British escort, the frigate *Minerva,* came down from the head of the convoy. Porter, longing for battle, flew the American colors and challenged the *Minerva.* The Englishman, however, refused the challenge, rounded up his convoy and made off. In this move he was quite correct, as British navy captains generally are. To be sure, he had lost one ship, but he had several more in his charge and it was his duty to protect them, not to meet the enemy on the field of honor like a medieval armored knight on horseback who is challenged by another knight. He sailed away, leaving one ship to his enemy. Had the *Essex* defeated him, the entire convoy would have been lost. This captured troopship was afterward ransomed for $14,000.

Before this two-month cruise was over, the *Essex* had one more great moment. She was mogging along, disguised as a merchantman, when the British sloop of war *Alert,* sixteen guns, gave chase. The *Essex* at this time carried forty thirty-two-pound carronades, short-barreled guns that could give a powerful blow at close quarters, but had nowhere near the range of the long guns. He also had six long twelve-pounders. Porter had protested bitterly to the Navy Department about this armament, but to no avail. He wanted long guns for his ship, but he did not get them, perhaps because the navy did not have them.

When she was built, the *Essex* had twenty-six long twelve-pounders, a battery that could not deliver really heavy blows, yet with good marksmanship was capable of putting up a good fight. Why the navy decided to put carronades on the *Essex,* thus making her incapable of engaging at long range an enemy carrying regular guns, is a mystery. Possibly it was thought that her captain would be clever enough to maneuver close to the enemy and fight a "yardarm to yardarm" battle. In such a fight, the thirty-two-pound carronades would certainly have been very effective, but whoever decreed an armament effective only in such a situation used questionable judgment, to say the least.

As the *Alert* stood down toward what she took to be an armed merchantman, a situation developed which made it important whether the *Essex* carried long guns or carronades. As the *Alert* drew near, her crew gave three cheers and let fly with a broadside. Instantly the frigate's gun ports opened and a thunderous broadside roared forth. Then the gunners fired at will and eight minutes of punishment from the heavy thirty-two-pound balls sufficed to reduce the Britisher to a sinking condition.

It was said that after the first broadside from the *Essex,* some of the English sailors deserted their guns and ran aft to beseech the captain to surrender the ship. Surrender the ship he did, when he saw his vessel was in danger of sinking. All

hands became prisoners of war. Later, after they were ex-
changed, several of those who deserted their guns were
brought to trial for cowardice, convicted and executed. This
is in complete accord with the doctrine of Britain's Royal
Navy. No sailor may desert his post no matter what punishment he is taking. Possibly he may die at his post, but posi-
tively he will be executed if he deserts it. Thus are men made
brave.

Now the *Essex* was loaded with hundreds of English prisoners as she headed back to the United States. Knowing, as
we do, that Englishmen never give up, it is not surprising
that a plot was hatched for a rising of the prisoners that
would result in the capture of the frigate. One of the leaders
in this affair was a coxswain in the *Alert*'s crew. Pistol in
hand, he tiptoed through the quarters of the midshipmen to
make sure they were all sleeping soundly. They were all
asleep, except a thirteen-year-old named David Glasgow Farragut, a lad who was destined to be heard of later on.

Young Farragut, seeing the pistol and recognizing the
fellow as a British prisoner, pretended to be asleep. When the
man was gone, David Farragut slipped out of his hammock,
raced aft to the captain's cabin and notified Porter. Alert-
ness and quickness of response in his crew were qualities
Captain Porter never ceased working toward. One of his dis-
ciplines was frequent fire drills, often made realistic by
buckets of burning rope and oakum in the hatches to create
clouds of realistic smoke. The crew had thus learned to make
a response that would gratify the chief of any modern big-
city fire department.

When the breathless young midshipman Farragut brought
him the message, Captain Porter bounded to the door of his

cabin and bellowed the fire call. Instantly all hands of the watch on deck came running aft, and the watch below tumbled out to join them. At his order his men took muskets, cutlasses and boarding pikes from the racks, and with Porter at their head, the English prisoners who were on the loose were rounded up, disarmed and clapped into irons.

This cruise ended September 7, 1812. To the *Essex* went the distinction of the first capture of an enemy merchantman and the further distinction of a successful cruise and the defeat of an enemy man-of-war. She refitted and took aboard stores. Then came orders to join the frigate *Constitution* and the sloop of war *Hornet* in the South Atlantic for a cruise to the Indian Ocean, there to attack the vessels of the East India Company, probably the richest trade in the world.

Calling at Port Praya in the Cape Verde Islands off the African coast, the *Essex* failed to make contact with the other vessels, nor did she find them at Fernando de Noronha. She made a capture at this time of the British packet ship *Nocton*. Putting a prize crew aboard, Porter ordered her to the United States. She nearly made it, but was captured by a British frigate off Bermuda.

Cruising off the Brazilian coast, hoping to fall in with the *Constitution* and the *Hornet,* Porter heard they had been engaged with the enemy and then had sailed north. The *Constitution* had indeed been engaged, for it was at this time she met the British frigate *Java* and defeated her in a furious battle. For some reason her captain decided to return to the United States. Captain Porter, upon hearing the report that both American vessels had sailed north, concluded that this left him free to evolve a new war plan of his own.

He thereupon decided to round Cape Horn to conduct a campaign against British commerce in the Pacific.

The decision to sail into an ocean where no American warship had ever operated was a serious one, for there the *Essex* would be beyond any help or support from any American port or ship. Captain David Porter, however, was a careful and resourceful commander who at all times had in mind every factor in any situation. One of his chief concerns was the health of his crew, and to this problem he applied methods unusual in that day but now recognized as extremely important.

He always laid in extra supplies of vegetables and fruit when he was in port. For the time when these perishables had been consumed he had lime juice for issue to the men. This is a preventive against scurvy, the disabling and sometimes fatal disease resulting from vitamin deficiency. Upon leaving port each mess was provided with as many pigs and poultry as could be accommodated in pens on deck, so that fresh meat was available for a while before falling back on salt beef and salt pork, the inevitable rations for a ship long at sea. Captain Porter was willing to put up with the untidiness incident to animals on the deck of his ship in order to have the beneficial results of fresh meat on the health of his crew.

When possible he cut the bread ration in half, issuing instead a half pound of potatoes or of apples, thus introducing more vitamins into the diet. Cleanliness and care of clothing were emphasized. The men were encouraged to bathe every day, and the captain directed that, in order to provide the men a good example, the officers were to take daily baths.

Every morning the ship was fumigated by heating cannon

balls red hot and then pouring vinegar on them. The men on watch were to be kept occupied with some sort of work at all times, but Captain Porter instructed his officers that the men were not to be harassed during their watch below by unnecessary calls of "All hands." From four to six in the afternoon watch was amusement time, and according to Captain Porter's orders, the officers were to see to it that the men were amused, just as they were to provide them with work during the watch on deck.

The crew were mustered every morning and given a "strict" examination by the officers. The men were to be guarded against unnecessary exposure to the weather. Porter believed in fresh air. He let the men sleep on the gun deck so they would have the benefit of air from the open gun ports. Seamen sleeping on the gun deck would have horrified any other navy captain, but what bothered Porter more was the "pernicious vapors" or the crowded and unventilated berth deck. Here again he was far ahead of his time, for in later years a fresh-air program such as this was adopted as one of the methods of preventing tuberculosis.

Once Captain Porter had made up his mind to cruise in the Pacific, he headed south along the coasts of Brazil and the Argentine Republic. The weather became steadily colder and the seas rougher. By early February he was in the area of Cape Horn, the dreaded "Cape Stiff" which every mariner hates, for it is probably the meanest and stormiest sea on the face of the globe.

A glance at the map will show how much further Cape Horn, the tip of South America, reaches toward the cold southern region of Antarctica than does the Cape of Good Hope, Africa's most southern point. Good Hope is a pleasant and livable climate, well populated and with important cities such as Capetown. Cape Horn is a cold and barren hell in a land of storm and frigid weather even in summer.

The frigate *Essex,* as does every ship, had a miserable time of it weathering Cape Horn, which it rounded February 14, 1813. Then, as with every vessel, the situation improved for the storm-battered frigate as she sailed northward along the coast of Chile. Now she bore the distinction of being the first American man-of-war ever to round Cape Horn, as well as the first to double the Cape of Good Hope. Putting in at Valparaiso, the *Essex* repaired the damage to sails and cordage resulting from her stormy passage, took on water and fresh provisions and gave the men rest and shore leave.

Departing from Valparaiso, the frigate commenced one of the most extraordinary adventures of any warship, sail or steam. This vessel, built of the white oak of Essex County, Massachusetts, ruled the entire Pacific, the world's largest ocean. Her dominion lasted over a year. It was a vigorous and relentless rule, which resulted in turning the vast reaches from Cape Horn to Alaska and from the Americas to Asia into an American lake.

The United States at this time was a small nation, unsure of its authority even in parts of the Mississippi Valley. The area which is now California was Spanish; Oregon and Washington and British Columbia were Indian country; Alaska was Russian. Yet the Pacific seas in the year 1813 were American, presided over by Captain David Porter of the United States Navy.

The rule of the *Essex* commenced not long after her departure from Valparaiso. She came up with the Peruvian vessel *Nereyda,* fifteen guns, a privateer, which Captain Porter proceeded to examine. Below decks were American seamen, held prisoners, and it soon appeared that this vessel had been cruising against American whaling ships, thinking this to be an easy way to make money. The Americans were immediately taken aboard the *Essex*. By way of showing disapproval of such conduct, Porter ordered all of the *Nereyda*'s guns and ammunition hove overboard. He then wrote a letter to the Governor General of Peru, stating that if any other of his corsairs or privateers were caught meddling with American ships, they would not get off as easily. Later the *Essex* recaptured one of the American vessels made prize by the Peruvian corsairs.

The frigate then began to round up British whaling ships operating in the Pacific. On April 29 three of them, *Montezuma, Georgianna* and *Policy,* all of them armed with cannon, were taken. On May 29 the frigate captured the *Atlantic* and the *Greenwich,* which had a plentiful supply of fresh water in her casks and eight hundred live tortoises which were a valuable supply of fresh meat for the American crew that had been living on salt horse and ship's biscuit.

In June the *Georgianna,* which Porter had armed and manned as an auxiliary, took the British ships *Catherine, Hector* and *Rose.* By now prisoners were so numerous as to become a problem, so the *Rose* was designated a "cartel." Seventy-three captive Britishers were put aboard and they were directed to sail around Cape Horn and make for the British island of St. Helena in the South Atlantic.

The captured ship *Atlantic,* being one hundred tons larger than the *Georgianna,* was now made the auxiliary to the *Essex.* She was armed with twenty guns taken from the various prizes, rechristened *Essex Junior* and became the second ship of the squadron. The *Greenwich* was made a store ship, for the Americans, now half a world away from any base of their own, were literally living off the enemy and needed a means of carrying the supplies they had captured.

In July the American squadron picked up the British *Charlton, New Zealander* and *Seringapatum.* The *Charlton* was sent to Rio de Janeiro with forty-eight more prisoners; the *Georgianna,* with an American crew, was loaded with captured whale oil and sent to the United States with this valuable cargo. In September the *Essex* captured a twelve-gun British letter of marque vessel, the *Sir Andrew Hammond,* bringing to twelve the number of enemy vessels taken in the Pacific. The *New Zealander* also was sent home with a full cargo of captured whale oil in November 1813. Such a cargo was worth a fortune and this was the second one that the *Essex* had sent back to the United States—oil that the captured British whaling ships had accumulated in a year or more of pursuing and killing these giant creatures, cutting them up and processing their blubber in the try kettles.

By this time the frigate *Essex* had practically destroyed the English whaling industry in the Pacific. Twelve ships had been captured, and with the spread of the news all other British vessels stayed in port so as not to fall victim to the American raider. The operations of the *Essex* had the further effect of making this entire ocean safe for Yankee whaling ships, which were able to go about their business, now for the first time free of the fear that one of the British whalers, all of which were well armed with cannon, might descend upon them.

By December Captain Porter knew that his ship must have

a thorough refit and have her bottom cleaned and the crew must be given shore leave somewhere with a change of diet and fresh food. To go to a South American port and dismantle his ship would leave her certain prey to any British warship that turned up while she was in a helpless condition. Porter was not so inexperienced as to suppose that the British did not know that he had practically swept their commerce from this vast ocean. Neither did he think for one moment that the English Lords of the Admiralty would fail to do something about it. Unless things in Britain had changed a great deal, at least one of His Majesty's men-of-war was on its way to deal with the *Essex*.

To accomplish this repair in undisturbed seclusion, Captain Porter ordered his fleet to sail three thousand miles west to the South Sea island of Marquesas. He arrived at the harbor of Nukuhiva with his frigate and the *Essex Junior* and the captured *Seringapatum, Greenwich* and *Sir Andrew Hammond*. In this beautiful island paradise the frigate was completely renovated and the men rehabilitated with plenty of shore leave to spend with the friendly native population. To guard against surprise, the Americans built a fort at the harbor entrance and mounted cannon from the captured vessels.

At last it was time to go and regretfully the men said good-by to friendly and beautiful Nukuhiva, where life seemed so easy. The three captured whalers were left there, guarded by the fort now manned by a marine officer and a garrison of twenty-three men. Captain Porter laid a course for Valparaiso.

Here is one of the mysteries of the remarkable cruise of the frigate *Essex*. Valparaiso is the first port of call for any vessel which has rounded Cape Horn. Therefore any British warship coming out from England to search for the notorious Yankee raider would be sure to look in there. Indeed, there is some reason to believe that Porter went to Valparaiso in the hope he would meet the English man-of-war sent to deal with him.

From today's viewpoint we find this difficult to understand. The *Essex*, a fast sailer, could have gone from one place to another in the wide reaches of the Pacific, eluding the British warships, destroying more of their merchantmen and disrupting their commerce indefinitely. Furthermore, the *Essex* was not properly armed for a real fight. Well did Porter know this, for he had protested at the short-range carronades he had and asked for long guns. He did not get them. The vessels he had captured carried several dozen guns. None of these were mounted on the *Essex,* doubtless because they were light four- and six-pounders of little use in a hard-fought action between warships.

Why then did Porter practically seek out an action with the enemy? Only one answer seems reasonable. The men of that day were much nearer the traditions of the medieval days of chivalry. The code of honor of those olden days had much more influence than we of today can realize. It was a time when duels were frequent. Challenges were sent over fancied insults and points of "honor" that seem preposterous to us; men met at dawn at some secluded spot, hot lead flew, and many a good man was pronounced dead by the surgeon always in attendance at such affairs. These duels were part of medieval tradition. In those days one armored knight met another. Both mounted on horseback, they charged at each other, lances leveled and sometimes, when both were knocked off their horses, they fought it out on foot with battle axes, swords and daggers.

In the War of 1812 there are several instances where one frigate challenged another, just as if they were two armored knights eager to meet upon the field of honor. Some of these challenges were in writing, some were oral. Both the British and the American naval officers were men of great courage, deeply imbued with the ideas of chivalric combat. It may be that such notions in Porter's mind overcame the excellent judgment that usually characterized his every action and led him to seek battle when he knew he did not have the armament to match a frigate with long guns. Perhaps he hoped to so maneuver the *Essex* as to come alongside the enemy, board her and fight it out on her decks with his superbly trained Yankee crew.

The event was different. Soon after the *Essex* reached Valparaiso, the British frigate *Phoebe* and the sloop of war *Cherub* appeared. One day the *Essex* challenged the *Phoebe*, which was patrolling outside the harbor, with the *Cherub* at a distance. The *Essex* sailed out to meet the *Phoebe*, which promptly ran to join the *Cherub* so they would be two to one, and the disappointed Captain Porter turned back into the harbor. What he did not know was that the Lords of the Admiralty at London, after the resounding defeats administered to British frigates by the *Constitution* and the *United States*, had completely abandoned the ancient notions of chivalry. Orders had been issued that no British frigate was to tackle an American frigate alone, so challenges by Captain Porter or anyone else were no longer anything but an anachronism.

Britain, no matter what romantic notions some of her

subjects may entertain, has always been a very practical nation. Her objective was control of the seas, and if to achieve
that two of her warships must be assigned to deal with one
American, then that was the way it would be done. The
Admiralty did not delude itself that the Royal Navy was
engaged in a tournament with anyone. They were fighting
so Britannia would rule the waves. So when the *Essex* sailed
out to do battle, the *Phoebe* fled from the disgusted Captain
Porter and joined the *Cherub*.

For four weeks the two English ships watched the *Essex*.
When word reached Porter that four more British men-of-
war were on the way to join in the pursuit of his vessel, he
realized that the days of challenges and single-ship combats
were indeed gone. Then followed some foul luck. An easterly
gale came up, and one of the American frigate's anchors
dragged. Porter decided to run for it, and the *Essex* went
bowling out of Valparaiso harbor. The gale was too much
for the sail she was carrying, however, and her main topmast
went by the board, carrying with it the topmen, who were
lost in the turbulent waters.

The *Essex* put back into the harbor, seeking a cove a half
mile from shore in which to make repairs, and the British
followed her in.

The *Phoebe* stayed away from the muzzles of the thirty-
two-pound carronades, so deadly at short range. Her captain
took a position beyond the reach of the carronades, yet
within range of her own long eighteen-pounders. There, on
March 28, 1814, the battle commenced in the neutral harbor
of Valparaiso.

The *Essex* had six long twelve-pounders that would reach
and she fought this battle with them alone. The *Phoebe*'s

twenty-six long eighteen-pounders kept up a steady fire on the *Essex*, the superiority of which was overwhelming, and the *Cherub* added a little. The American twelve-pounders were well served. They marked up the *Phoebe* considerably and drove off the *Cherub*, yet the British superiority of gun-fire could have but one final result. On one of the twelve-pounders three complete crews, fifteen men, became casualties.

Captain Porter and his men endured this hail of cannon balls for two and a half hours. He tried to make sail to close with *Phoebe*, but the storm of shot had so disabled his rigging that the frigate would not sail. He tried to run his vessel ashore so he might let his men escape on land, but his disabled ship could not make it. He told those who could swim to try for the shore. Some made it, and some drowned or were captured, but most of them elected to remain with him until the bitter end.

Finally he knew he must surrender, for of a crew of 255 men, only 75 were now fit for duty. He had lost 58 killed and 66 wounded. The surgeons worked below in the cockpit on the casualties, and enemy shot came tearing through the sides of the frigate, killing men even as their wounds were being dressed. The decks, rigging and spars of the *Essex* were one great heap of kindling wood from the dreadful hammering of British eighteen-pound shot. So at last the *Essex* frigate lowered her colors and surrendered.

Captain Porter was in tears as his flag floated down to the deck. He had a great deal to say about this enemy who attacked him in a neutral harbor. This was a breach of international law, however, that meant nothing to the British. The government of Chile, a nation recently freed from Spanish rule, was in no position to make trouble for mighty

England, mistress of the seas, and the *Phoebe*'s Captain Hill-yar well knew this. The British objective, command of the seas, had been achieved inexpensively; their casualties were but five dead and seven wounded from the American twelve-pounders. No more would English shipping in the Pacific be troubled by the *Essex*. That ocean had ceased to be an American lake; it was again an English lake.

The English captain, however, was a gentleman in one respect. To be sure, he had made certain that both of his warships attacked the *Essex* at once, he had waited until her main topmast had carried away before he would fight, and he had violated the neutrality of the Chilean republic. Yet he was generous to the men of the *Essex*, now she was defeated. He made the *Essex Junior* into a cartel, put the American crew aboard her and permitted them to sail for the United States with a letter from him assuring them safe passage home.

When not far from New York, the *Essex Junior* was halted by the British man-of-war *Saturn*, whose commander questioned Captain Hillyar's authority to give safe conduct. While the *Saturn*'s captain was pondering this problem a heavy fog came up and the impatient Captain Porter ordered a boat put over the side, took a dozen of his men and rowed away into the dense blanket of white. They landed on Long Island, drove to New York, and there they met their comrades, for the *Essex Junior* had finally been released by the *Saturn*'s puzzled captain and had sailed into port.

At Valparaiso, after the departure of the *Essex Junior*, the British had on their hands the captured American frigate, a vessel now in a sad state from the pounding she had taken. They plugged the shot holes, pumped her out and repaired the yards, masts and rigging until again she was seaworthy. She was taken into the Royal Navy, but what service she performed for England was not significant enough to be recorded. In 1837 the British disposed of her.

What happened to the *Essex* after March 28, 1814, is of no real interest to Americans, for it was on that day she died. The fabric of the ship, made of good Essex County oak, continued to exist, but its soul had departed, and whether the English had her or who had her or what use was made of her attracted no notice. For Americans she was gone, but what she did while the national colors whipped in the breeze from her halyards was not gone; it was told over and over by Yankee sailor men when they met together and by people ashore.

The *Essex* lived on in the oceans where all alone she did her great deeds. In the war with Japan one of America's aircraft carriers bore the name *Essex,* and she lived up to the reputation of the old frigate. More carriers were built on her model, known as the "Essex class," and one by one they joined the fleet. In the enormous armada America finally assembled to fight Japan, the *Essex* class carriers did their part in making the Pacific Ocean an American lake as it had not been since that time in 1813 and 1814 when it was ruled throughout its great extent by one frigate, the frigate that was built in Salem.

16 ⌇⌇

The Ice King

THOSE STRANGE PEOPLE called the Yankees for centuries have inhabited the cold northeast corner of these United States, a region without coal or oil or iron or any other natural resources except water power, granite and themselves. One sage old Yankee observed that had the settlement of North America commenced at the West Coast, New England would have little in it except a few railroad lines running from the rest of the country to the seaports. Because he lives in a region with which Mother Nature dealt so stingily, the New Englander has, through the centuries, learned to make the very best of what little he has.

Other parts of the country gather the riches of the earth. They harvest crops from boundless acres of black soil. They mine coal and copper, silver and gold, and drill in oil fields where a fortune awaits luck and skill and persistence. Lands of tall timber, of vast herds of cattle and sheep, golden wheat, fields where the furrow is a mile long—all these lie beyond the boundaries of New England.

And a great part of these lands have been developed by Yankees who long ago, or perhaps but yesterday, could see the opportunities to the west and drove on toward the setting sun. Maybe he sat the seat of his covered wagon, his rifle on his knees, guiding his two yoke of oxen. Or perhaps he arrived last month, stepping off a train of the Union Pacific or the Santa Fe or from a plane at the airport of some western town.

Yankees started going West long ago. They were on the way before the Revolution and were fighting the Indians and the French under the officers of the British King in the long struggles for Pittsburgh and Detroit. No phase of the westward expansion of the United States was without them. They and their descendants are everywhere, all the way to the Pacific Coast. But New England never ran empty. Many stayed in this land of thin topsoil and sparse mineral wealth. By their labors and their qualities, New England became a place of fine workmanship, of invention, superb education at all levels, the part of the country where interesting ideas grew and flourished. It has always been the place where folks do the best they can with what they have.

Not in the more than three centuries that civilized man has been on these shores has anyone made more interesting use of what lies at hand than Frederic Tudor of Boston. His story begins in 1805 with an odd idea in the head of a youth twenty-two years old, an idea combined with stubborn persistence and ingenuity.

This idea may have come to him on one of those cold, clear days in middle or late January, a day when the glass had been zero at dawn and possibly edged up to eighteen by noon. Such days do not come to New England singly. They come in succession, when the northwest wind has rolled the accumulated cold of the Arctic Circle down upon us for several days and the best place to be is in the kitchen near a stove well stoked with oak and maple.

Those are the days when the ice in the ponds grows thicker until it will easily bear the weight of a horse. Many a farmer in the old days would cut a few dozen cakes of ice on his pond, stow them away in a little cavelike excavation dug into a side hill, cover them with hay and shut tight the door. Then in summer he would have ice to keep meat and other foods from spoiling and a few pieces to put into his switchel jug when he went haying beneath the broiling summer sun.

It may have been his brother William who entertained himself with the thought of how much the rich planters on the islands of the West Indies would enjoy a cake of ice a foot or more in thickness from one of the ponds of New England. Here it lay, countless acres of thick ice on the numerous ponds, a very little of it used by some nearby farmer who had a tiny icehouse for his own needs.

"Think how nice it would be," observed William Tudor, "for some planter coming into his house after a hot morning riding around his plantation to look over his fields of sugar cane and to see that his men were attending to his work, if he could sit down to a long, tall, cool drink with ice tinkling in his glass. Probably he has never seen ice, and look how much we have here."

Frederic Tudor did not miss a word.

"If we could only export some of the month of January," continued William. And after his fanciful remarks William forgot about the subject and turned to something else.

Frederic Tudor, however, did not forget about it. He turned it over in his mind, again and again, thinking out each step necessary to bring cakes of Massachusetts ice into the markets of the West India islands, where planters grew wealthy raising tropical produce such as sugar and coffee in broad and fertile fields tilled by black slaves who could stand the labor in the heat of these lands. These European owners were wealthy, but the price they paid was life in an oppressively hot and pestilential climate. Tudor figured that anything making existence more bearable in the perpetual heat would be worth good money anywhere in the islands. He determined to send a shipload of ice to Martinique, a prosperous French island where only recently the scourge of yellow fever had struck.

From a pond in that part of Lynn, Massachusetts, later known as Saugus, he had one hundred and thirty tons of ice cut. When he tried to arrange for transportation of his ice to Martinique, he found no shipowner willing to accept such a cargo for fear the ice would melt faster than the vessel's pumps could take care of the water and the ship would founder. So Frederic Tudor purchased the brig *Favorite* and commenced carting the ice from its place of storage in the Saugus part of Lynn to the pier in Boston where his ship lay.

When people in Boston's business world learned that this young man intended to load a vessel with ice for the West Indies, there was great merriment. Tudor was ridiculed, but this troubled him not at all. Throughout his long life he preserved a complete disregard of the opinions of others if he were firmly convinced he was right. And in this episode another characteristic is quite plain; he had the capability of translating ideas into action.

The voyage of the brig *Favorite* to Martinique with its cargo was a modified success. The ice did not melt and carry the vessel to the bottom, and the planters received this new product with enthusiasm. Here again Frederic Tudor's planning was excellent, for he had sent brother William and James Savage ahead to receive the cargo when it arrived, to act as salesmen and show the people how to mix cold drinks American style. In spite of careful planning, however, Frederic Tudor lost $4500 on this expedition to Martinique. The loss was not caused by lack of appreciation on the part of customers. To the contrary, the well-to-do people were delighted with this excellent variation in the tedious life of a sun-baked sugar island, and those who had suffered from yellow fever and had survived found the cold drinks very satisfying.

The loss resulted from the plain fact that there were not enough tall glasses on Martinique to use the one hundred and thirty tons of ice before it melted. The customers cheerfully bought ice while it lasted, and when it was gone, mostly through melting, they watched the brig sail away, hoping for her return with more blocks of New England January. As for Frederic Tudor, his mind was at work, this time on a plan for constructing a building for storing ice in a tropical port. His was a problem of what today would be termed "insulation engineering."

As Frederic Tudor contemplated the Martinique venture, he showed a bit of the granite that is built into so many Yankees. These are the words he wrote in his journal: "He who gives back at the first repulse and without striking the second blow despairs of success, has never been, is not, and never will be a hero in love, war or business."

He persisted and by his ingenuity he perfected the technical details of keeping ice in the tropics until it was time to sell it to planters and to coffee shops. He double-sheathed his ships so the heat did not penetrate the hold. He had the captain make sure the hatches were never removed so warm air could be admitted. After experimenting with rice chaff, wheat chaff, hay, coal dust and tan bark, he chose pine sawdust as the most efficient insulating agent. This he packed between the double sheathing of his ships, on top of the ice cargo and in the double walls of the ice storage houses he built in the ports of the West Indies.

As important as any technique of preserving ice was his thorough study of salesmanship to make his ice move fast after the arrival of the cargo. He introduced ice in hospitals in hot-weather countries by giving generous free samples. He promoted the establishment of ice cream shops. The rum shops frequented by the poor received his most diligent sales efforts and were given plenty of free samples. His theory was that even the poor, once introduced to a cold drink, would from then on consider Yankee ice essential to their refreshment. He gave his customers free instructions in the art of keeping ice from melting once they got it home. This required considerable teaching, for these people were completely unfamiliar with the characteristics of ice. One customer left his block on the front doorstep in the sun and then wondered what had become of it.

Tudor even managed to persuade the Brazilian government, on grounds of public health, to remit import duties on the cargoes of his ships. Over the years from 1805 to 1812 he succeeded in building up a solvent ice business in the West Indies and South America. Then came the war with Britain in 1812; American commerce was swept from the seas, and the ice business ceased to exist.

However, with the Peace of Ghent in 1815, which ended

our war with England, the alert Frederic Tudor was ready with more ice ventures. From our recent enemies, the British, he obtained permission to build icehouses in Kingston, Jamaica, and other British ports and he was given a monopoly of the business.

He set up icehouses in Charleston, South Carolina, in New Orleans and in Havana as well as in the West Indies and South America. At times he did well and considered himself rich. At other times he suffered reverses so serious that he was arrested for debt on several occasions.

One of these setbacks resulted from thievery by his trusted manager of the Havana icehouse. This fellow, whom Tudor had taken from a poorly paid job and elevated to an excellent position, was seized with the urge to progress even faster, so he emptied the Tudor cash register in Havana and decamped.

Another crisis resulted from one of New England's infrequent mild winters. Doubtless most Yankees were happy with weather in January mild enough so that a man did not want to keep his feet in the oven. That year there was open water in the ponds all winter. For the ice merchants this was ruinous. The determined Tudor solved the problem expensively by sending his crews to the upper Kennebec in Maine. This was costly, but he was still in the ice business.

Then, on another occasion, this high-strung man had a nervous collapse that removed him from the business arena for a long time. A bachelor then, he had no one to care for him until his brother-in-law, Robert Hallowell Gardiner, took charge and carefully nursed him back to health.

That a man whose chief business was selling ice should like winter is in no way surprising. On one occasion, after concluding satisfactorily a piece of business in Cuba, he committed to his journal these words: "Thus is the winter of my discontent made glorious summer. Drink, Spaniard, and be cool, that I who have suffered much in the cause may be able to go home and keep myself warm." Again at his home in Boston, he reached for his journal on a cold January night and wrote: "The frost covers the windows, the wheels creak, the boys run, winter rules, and fifty thousand dollars worth of ice floats for me upon Fresh Pond."

Not only did he harvest ice from Fresh Pond in Cambridge, but Spot Pond in Stoneham, Smith's Pond and Walden Pond in Concord were part of his system. His ice operations at Walden Pond were conducted at the time that a Yankee named Henry David Thoreau lived a solitary and philosophical life in a cabin on the shore, filling notebooks with platitudes, observations of nature and comments on such aspects of life as came within his view.

Thoreau was much taken with the thought that the ice Tudor's men were cutting on Walden Pond was to be transported to such far places, and his journal received the benefit of his observations on this subject. Thoreau wrote: "The sweltering inhabitants of Charleston and New Orleans, Madras, Bombay and Calcutta drink at my well." To this straightforward statement he added numerous remarks full of appropriate classical references.

Frederic Tudor's worst ordeal resulted from his effort to be more like other businessmen. His ice enterprises were completely unique. He felt too much apart from other men of affairs, so he decided upon a venture closer to those in which other Boston merchants were engaged. He started trading in coffee in 1834. His successes in speculation were immediate and so gratifying that he was tempted to extend his operations.

He went into this project with great thoroughness, so that when a drop in coffee prices occurred and the market crashed, he was in a serious position. By the time he had liquidated his coffee operations and settled up, he was in debt to the extent of $210,000. Many a man in such an embarrassed condition has gone through insolvency or bankruptcy proceedings. This thought never occurred to Frederic Tudor. His way was to see all his creditors and ask them to leave him alone until he could earn enough to pay them in full.

Pay in full he did and with interest. It took until 1849, a period of fifteen years, but no one lost a cent. He recovered himself by strict attention to the ice business. It was after his coffee disaster that he sent his first cargo of ice to Calcutta. This new market prospered. In 1836 he shipped 12,000 tons to India and in 1846, 65,000 tons.

To reach India before the existence of the Suez Canal required crossing the equator twice. Such was the technique used by Tudor that his ships got through all this hot weather with little loss of ice. The British in Calcutta welcomed the frigid cargoes enthusiastically and some of the products packed in with the ice, such as Baldwin apples. They even built icehouses for him.

Competition followed Tudor wherever he went. There were at least a dozen other ice companies in the business, yet he managed to stay ahead of them all. The most well known of his competitors was the company that exported Wenham Lake ice, a clear and pure product that became world famous. Rudyard Kipling in his *Second Jungle Book* describes the adjutant bird on a pier in Calcutta that saw a piece of Wenham Lake ice from an American ice schooner and swallowed it. Then commenced for this tropical creature an entirely new experience, described as only the pen of Rudyard Kipling could do it.

It is often the case that a man of great capability turns his powers to more than one line of work. So it was with Frederic Tudor. Becoming interested in Nahant, an island lying a mile offshore from Lynn and reached by a road across a long sand spit over which the waves broke in a northeast storm, he purchased considerable land in this barren, wind-swept place. Natives of Nahant assured him nothing could be made to grow in this rocky soil where stormy gales and cold northwest winds took charge so much of the time.

Difficult problems did not bother Tudor; they exhilarated him. He planted many trees, arranging them so the stout and hardy ones formed windbreaks to protect the more delicate varieties. In the shelter of tall fences to break the force of the winds that blew across the island, he planted gardens, fruit trees and even wheat successfully.

In 1858, after years of successful cultivation of his land, he held a garden party for his Nahant neighbors who had told him nothing would grow there. All the inhabitants of the town were invited. This was a festivity never to be for-gotten. He gave fruit and vegetables to each one of his guests. He made cider on the spot from his own apples, giving every-one a drink. Not only that, but everyone had a drink of "perry," an uncommon beverage made from the juice of pears.

After his successes with farm and orchards, Tudor bought several acres on the north shore of Nahant in 1859. He needed more land; he had another idea. Situated near popu-lous Boston and the busy shoe-manufacturing city of Lynn,

Nahant, he decided, was exactly the place for a public amusement park. This was a new idea in 1859, and his was one of the first in the country.

Tudor named this new project Maolis Gardens. Enclosing the park with a high slatted fence, he planted flower beds and built sheltered summerhouses, swings, tilts, an ice cream pavilion, a bear den and cages for animals. There was a dance hall and at the edge of the cliff, looking down at the waves breaking on the rugged rocks of the shore, there was an outdoor dining room.

Here and there about the park were outdoor stoves to be rented to those who wished to cook their own dinners alfresco, and a plentiful pile of split driftwood was provided free with each stove. Maolis Gardens had a teahouse and a marble temple, flying horses, a wheel of fortune, a target range, croquet games, a Punch-and-Judy show, Indians selling baskets and two trained bears. The concessionaires included a "balloon man" (who sold toy balloons), a "candy man" and a "tintype man" who could take a photograph (provided the subject sat still long enough), which finally appeared on a thin piece of tin which was delivered to the customer.

Admission to this astonishing collection of delights was five cents for adults and three cents for children. A steamboat left India Wharf in Boston for Nahant three times a day. As for the Lynn trade, they came over the road across the mile-long sand spit in horse-drawn "barges," long vehicles with a bench on each side running lengthwise. These were the predecessors of today's motorbus, and the sandy road is now replaced by a fine modern motor road. However, when a storm is raging on the Atlantic, this modern road is a very wet place to be. As for Maolis Gardens, it is now filled with neat rows of houses and the memory of it lives in the name of one of the streets.

Frederic Tudor was a pioneer in the overseas ice trade, a business in which he was followed by many capable merchants. Ice came to be one of the port of Boston's most important exports, the high point being in 1860, when 142,463 tons were shipped to over fifty different destinations.

Probably of all the ventures which followed Tudor's lead, the most interesting was the exporting of Wenham Lake ice all over the world. It was Wenham Lake ice that Kipling's adjutant bird swallowed and it was Wenham Lake ice that became such a favorite in London that fine hotels and restaurants advertised that they used it. Its superiority even became the subject of scientific investigation, as various learned men, among them Faraday, undertook to discover why it did not melt as fast as English ice and why it was so much clearer.

The merchants who sold it did their best to make their product interesting. One method was to select a particularly clear block of ice, bore a hole in it, drop in a pickerel, then pour water into the hole and let it freeze. This, when shipped to England, made a prime exhibit for the window of some fancy restaurant that advertised it used Wenham Lake ice.

When Mr. Hittinger first went to London to try to open a market for Wenham Lake ice, he saw the proper parties and managed to get permission to offer his product at a large gathering of the Fishmongers' Association. He hired bartenders and trained them in mixing iced drinks. There was a moment of silence as the Englishmen tried something new, then there were comments of a very unappreciative nature about the iced drinks. Hittinger, when he reached America, attempted to sum up the comments in one quotation. According to him, this is what one Englishman said:

"I say, aw, waitaw, a little 'ot wataw, if you please. I prefer it 'alf 'n 'alf."

Americans never tire of imitating the peculiarities of the British variety of the English language, and this is one of the early efforts. Mr. Hittinger, bitterly disappointed at the reception the English gave his ice, took the next boat home from Liverpool. However, as Frederic Tudor had said many years before, ice never succeeds at first. By his persistence he had shown people in many lands the uses of ice. So the Wenham Lake Company kept at it until they were rewarded by a tremendous acceptance of their product by the British public.

The ice trade did a great deal for American commerce. It provided winter employment for hundreds in the work of cutting and storing the blocks and in building storage houses. Many ships were employed and Americans made a lot of money selling this product of Yankee cold weather. When our trade with India was languishing, the ice shipments put new vigor into it.

What was probably the biggest moment for the men in the ice trade came in 1844 in the dead of winter. For nearly four years the new Cunard Line of steamships had made Boston the American terminus of their transatlantic runs. As might be expected, the New Yorkers did not approve at all. For nearly four years the New York newspapers had lost no opportunity to assert the shortcomings of Boston as the American end of the Cunard voyages, and every New Yorker joined the chorus.

In January of 1844 it appeared that New York had won

its point. It was one of the coldest months in Boston's history; the harbor froze solid all the way out to the islands, and the Cunarder *Britannia,* at her berth in Boston harbor, was completely frozen in. She was advertised to sail in three days, but there was a foot of ice in the harbor. The New York papers predicted the *Britannia* would be fortunate to be able to depart by St. Patrick's Day.

The Boston merchants had a meeting, and every man present knew how important a moment this was for his city. By unanimous vote they decided to cut a channel for the Cunarder. The New Yorkers scoffed. A channel must be several miles long and the ship was due to sail in three days.

The folks in the big town did not know about Frederic Tudor and the other Yankee icemen. Down to Boston harbor they came, hundreds of them, with their groovers and saws and all their bars and chisels, and they brought their horses, too. They worked day and night and they knew exactly what to do. The Cunarder sailed on time through a channel of free water miles long. All Boston turned out to see the *Britannia* depart and the long channel through the ice was lined with cheering thousands. No cheers, however, were heard from New York.

Frederic Tudor died in 1864, leaving a house on Beacon Street, Boston, and another in Nahant. He left a fortune and a great name of one who originated and dared to do and never gave up. One of the most significant memorials to this remarkable Yankee came in 1877, thirteen years after his death, when a ship built by the Tudor Ice Company especially to carry ice to the East Indies slid down the ways at East Boston. She was christened the *Ice King.* No one needed to ask for whom she was named.

Yet anyone who for a moment wondered had only to look at the expertly carved figurehead: a life-sized representation of Frederic Tudor, the Ice King of New England and the West Indies and Calcutta and two score palm-fringed harbors where the tropic heat is fierce, and the white man is perpetually weary and thirsty.

17 ⟿

The Captain's Gold

MOST OF WHAT we know about Captain Israel Foster we find in a law book, an old musty volume designated as *17 Massachusetts*. On page 479 et sequitur, in the opinion of the Justices of the Supreme Judicial Court, the story unfolds.

In June 1812 old Captain Foster had been ashore quite a while, living in a small house in Marblehead, near enough to the sea so he could watch the ships, the whitecaps when it was a bit rough and the long rollers when a real northeaster came howling across Salem Bay. In some ways life may have been harsh to him, for we know that in his old age he was living alone in the little house.

Yet we have the further knowledge that in material things life had been kind to him. Tucked away somewhere in his house the old mariner had a keg of gold pieces, Spanish doubloons, Portuguese moidores, English sovereigns, and the value of these coins in terms of American money was $53,-174.63. Whenever he needed something he reached a gold piece or two out of his keg and headed for the store. A doubloon was worth sixteen dollars, a moidore more than three dollars; at 1812 prices he never needed many coins to satisfy his needs.

Where did Captain Foster acquire this fortune? We come in near the end of his story and therefore we do not know exactly how he came by the money. Cynical people, whenever they hear of a Yankee fortune, are likely to say "black gold," which means the slave trade. This is an unfair assumption.

Few vessels on this coast ever carried slaves. In fact few Yankee mariners ever traded on the West African or "slave" coast for any purpose. Later, after the slave trade had long since ended, the Salem vessels carried on a brisk trade with Zanzibar on the East African coast. Americans also called at Capetown, usually for supplies and to swap merchandise, and they picked up many shipments of Ethiopian goatskins, with sometimes a leopard's hide somewhere in the bale. These skins were usually purchased at Aden from Arab traders.

A Yankee skipper who had made his pile, and many of them made much more than did Captain Israel Foster, usually had a long history of trading in the West Indies, the Mediterranean, Calcutta and Bombay or along the Sumatran coast. The ports of Europe, including Russia, saw American merchantmen with great frequency. The money was made in sugar, molasses, coffee and mahogany from the Caribbean, the pepper of Sumatra, the textiles of India, the wines, salt, fruits and luxuries of the Mediterranean and the manufactured products of Europe.

There Foster doubtless made his money, carefully laying it away in the form of gold pieces issued by nations whose coinage could be trusted. There is nothing in this world which has as interesting and at the same time as mysterious a career as a gold piece.

The coin is valuable, as everyone from a king to a cannibal

savage knows immediately. Thus the transactions in which it figures are important, sometimes so much so that murder is done. A gold coin has far journeys, for it is acceptable everywhere. And it has long rests, for it is of imperishable value, small in bulk, easy to store, ideal for the savings of a man like Captain Foster. The coins in his keg had led a quiet life for a long, long time, with only one of them, now and then, taken out for a trip to the store to pay for some provisions.

Yet a day came when Israel Foster's gold, all of it, fared forth on a journey. The reason was war. To the dismay of most New Englanders, the United States had declared war on England in June of 1812. The impetuous Westerners and Southerners, the "War Hawks," carried the nation into war; the merchant traders along the Yankee coast laid up their ships, and the fight was on.

It did not take Captain Foster long to figure out what would happen. An immediate British blockade stopped commerce and put all exposed parts of the coast at the mercy of landing parties from the King's ships. This meant that wherever the British landed there would be looting, burning and all the outrages which invading forces of that day felt was their just due whenever they were in enemy territory.

He had no intention of letting the fortune he had carefully accumulated throughout a lifetime at sea fetch up in the pockets of the thieving scum of the English water fronts, which was the element most likely to be found in any party set ashore by the Royal Navy to gather up supplies and teach the Yankees a lesson. So he lost no time in getting a horse and buggy to transport his keg of gold to the vaults of the Essex Bank of Salem, five miles away. There it would be safe from marauding landing parties of the British navy. Immediately the question arises: why should this property, which was in imminent danger in Marblehead, be safe in Salem? The answer lies partly in geography.

Marblehead is on a rocky cape on the outermost southern reaches of Salem Bay. Beyond is the broad Atlantic. Therefore a British man-of-war landing a raiding party could anchor a short distance offshore, send in the boats and be in no danger while awaiting their return. The British ship in this position was obliged to risk no navigational hazards and face no enemy action, for the fort guarding Marblehead faced Salem Bay and not the Atlantic Ocean.

But Salem, although only five miles from Marblehead, is not exposed to the open ocean. Lying at the western end of a bay which has numerous shoals, ledges and islands, it can be reached only by one or the other of two channels that require an expert local pilot at the helm. A vessel entering the South Channel would be obliged to pass within range of Fort Sewall, which stood at the mouth of Marblehead harbor, and then follow a difficult course within musket shot of the shore.

The local battery of field artillery would have excellent practice on a ship so near shore—a target difficult to miss. Marksmen with rifles would have at their mercy any sailor who went into the rigging to work ship in these narrow waters.

If the enemy attempted to enter by the Main Ship Channel on the other side of the bay, he would be under fire from the moment he passed between Baker's Island and Gale's Point in Manchester. This channel, near the wooded Beverly shore, would bring any British man-of-war under the steady fire of riflemen and field artillery.

By either route the enemy would finally reach Fort Pickering at the mouth of Salem harbor, there to come under the fire of its heavy guns. Should a British ship run aground anywhere in this bay, she would be helpless when the tide ebbed, leaving her canted to port or starboard on some ledge or sand bar.

Salem was safe, so there the keg stayed in the vault of the Essex Bank for the next two years.

The bank officers had counted the gold when the captain brought it in and had given him a receipt for $53,174.63. From time to time, as he needed money, he went over to get a few pieces, giving the bank a receipt each time.

As the war went on, the valiant American fleet with its two dozen ships put up some surprising battles against England's mighty navy. Yet in spite of proud victories, it was chased and harried by the superior numbers of the enemy. The Yankee coast was unprotected. So were the coasts of the other states. The British landed an army and burned the city of Washington. Two of their frigates pursued the *Constitution* into Marblehead harbor. Their *Shannon,* in a running battle from the outer reaches of Boston harbor to Thatcher's Island, pounded our frigate *Chesapeake* into a wreck.

If the British had an army to take Washington, might they not have a force to be landed anywhere along the shore that could march overland to capture Salem. Such a move was quite within the enemy's capability. The directors of the Essex Bank felt that even Salem, with its fort and its militia, was not a safe place for valuables. Therefore they decided to move the contents of their vault to Haverhill, which lies well up the Merrimac River.

No British ship could navigate this stream without a skilled local pilot. Even had the Royal Navy found some Yankee pilot whose palm could be crossed with gold, the banks of the Merrimac would have been lined with American sharpshooters who would have knocked the English sailors out of the rigging every time they attempted to make or take in sail.

Had the enemy tried to send an expedition upriver in ships' boats, cutters and pinnaces, the gunfire from the wooded banks would have decimated them. So the Salem people concluded their property was safe in Haverhill until such time as the enemy landed a military force to march up the valley of the Merrimac, very unlikely when many more profitable objectives lay along the coast.

A caravan of wagons went over the road from Salem to Haverhill bearing all the coin and specie of the Essex Bank and all the money, jewelry and silverware placed in its vaults by customers for safekeeping. Armed men rode the wagons, armed outriders went ahead and to the rear, armed men rode their horses through the dust at the sides of the creaking vehicles. Not only was the bank's property loaded in the wagons, but fine furniture, dishes, choice wines, and silverware from the mansions of Salem and bolts of silk from fashionable stores.

In 1815, when the war was ended, the valuables were transported back to Salem, again with a heavy armed guard, and life went on as usual. Captain Israel Foster, now really an old man, decided to leave his keg of gold pieces in the Essex Bank, from time to time making such withdrawals as his needs required.

Then, in 1818, three years later, the old mariner went to his last anchorage, and the executors of his will took over his affairs. With the receipt for $53,174.63 they headed for the Essex Bank, where they were shown the receipts Captain Foster had signed for the various amounts he had drawn since first he placed his money there for safekeeping. These totaled

$7625, so it was agreed that the executors were entitled to $45,549.63.

The bank officials produced the keg, and everyone sat down at a big mahogany table, lighted Manila cigars and in a genial and relaxed atmosphere commenced the counting. The atmosphere did not continue to be relaxed for long. When all the gold coins in the keg were counted and stacked on the table, the total was only $13,000. In the bottom part of the keg there lay not gold but pieces of iron ship ballast. When they were removed, the method of an extremely clever larceny stood revealed.

A piece of wood had been cut from the bottom of the keg, gold pieces had been abstracted, and ballast iron chunks had been thrust in to take the place of the stolen coins. All this was done so cleverly that the layer of doubloons, sovereigns and moidores on top was undisturbed. So with nimble fingers someone had managed to make himself $32,549 richer without anyone knowing what was going on.

It takes little effort to imagine the uproar this discovery caused in the Essex Bank. The investigation had not proceeded very far before it appeared that the cashier and the chief clerk of the bank had vanished. Then an audit was immediately ordered, which revealed that these two had falsified the books and purloined a sum of money so large that the solvency of the bank was impaired.

The story of these two men who betrayed their trust and made poorer so many people in their own home town is a sad one. Yet it is a story we have heard many times, before and since. Sheppard Gray and James King, the two bank employees who committed this crime, were men who loved luxurious living. Not only that, but they thought they had discovered an investment which would yield them very large profits.

They lived in fine houses and passed as rich men. Whenever there was a parade of the Salem Light Infantry, King entertained lavishly. In our more sophisticated day bank employees who lived in such princely style on modest salaries would soon be the subjects of a careful investigation. However, one hundred and fifty years ago American banking and business men did not have the careful methods which now are almost universal. So the directors and depositors of the Essex Bank drank James King's wine and visited in Sheppard Gray's beautiful house without ever pausing to wonder.

Investigation uncovered something else which has often resulted in the destruction of a man's honesty. They found these two had been putting money into an investment from which they expected to make a mint of money—the raising of merino sheep in Windsor, Vermont.

There were many who made a good thing in that day from sheep in Vermont. A glance into the state's history reveals enormous activity in sheep raising everywhere on those rugged hills, an activity that continued until better land and an easier climate farther west resulted in the migration of so many farmers.

Even though merino sheep raising was profitable, Sheppard Gray and James King lost the money they stole from Captain Foster and from the Essex Bank and invested in the enterprise. Two reasons for this loss immediately are suggested. They may have invested with someone as dishonest as themselves. Furthermore, no man's investment is safe if it is too far from its owner's supervision, unless it is in the hands of a very capable man, such as a sea captain who knows the trade route on which he sails.

So these two men fetched up in the hands of either a scoundrel or an incompetent, with the result that this money they had so ingeniously stolen completely vanished, along with their bright visions of making fortunes. However, not all the stolen money went into sheep. They had enough left so they were able to decamp to what in those days was called "Upper Canada."

This term meant anywhere beyond the settled regions along the St. Lawrence River and the shore of the Lakes. So they might have been in the rural parts of Ontario or they might have gone into the tundra of the frozen North among the Eskimos, there to look for gold the hard way. Of their life after leaving Salem we know little except that in Upper Canada they were safe, for the arm of Massachusetts law could not reach into this wilderness.

We do know that what gold they did not lose in the Vermont merino sheep transaction they managed to hold on to. And we know they did not like living in Upper Canada, for the Reverend William Bentley's diary on January 8, 1819, records that they offered $20,000 to settle the claim against them. This was one tenth of the loss, observed Bentley. It was not accepted.

The thievery of these two was so serious that it resulted in the insolvency of the Essex Bank. Not only did they wreck the bank, cause the stockholders to lose the value of stock which had been selling at $230 per share, and humiliate the directors and officials, but they brought shame to all of Salem, then one of the important cities of America. In his diary under the date of August 24, 1818, Bentley wrote: "Rather a wounding day to the pride of Salem."

The most direct and severe loss of all was suffered by the

legatees of the will of Israel Foster. Because of the drop in the quotation on Essex Bank stock the executors lost $2625.92 on the sale of Captain Foster's eighteen shares, according to the account they filed in the Probate Court. And according to their account, the value of the gold pieces stolen from the keg was $30,287.41.

The legatees, mostly nephews and nieces, were very much exasperated by this outrage. The real culprits were far beyond their reach, but they were determined to do something to someone, so they turned their wrath upon the Essex Bank, even though it was tottering on its foundations from the blow the thieves had struck it.

The executors, when they commenced court action, certainly sought excellent legal counsel, for there appears in their second account in the Registry of Probate at Salem this entry: "Paid Daniel Webster, Esqr, Fees on Bank suit $75." This suit was on the theory that the Essex Bank was negligent in its care of the keg of gold entrusted to it by Captain Foster and therefore liable for the damage that resulted; to wit, $30,287.41.

This case went all the way to the full bench of the Supreme Judicial Court, and a lengthy opinion was written, which appears in Volume 17 of the *Massachusetts Reports* at page 479. The Court decided the bank was not liable.

What these two employees did was not done in any way in the course of their duties. A bank is answerable for the correct conduct of all its servants in their proper sphere of duty. If an employee's character is such that he commits a crime like this, the bank is not liable. It is something unforeseeable. So the Essex Bank was not responsible for the loss occasioned by the felonies of these two rascals, and all the eloquent arguments of Daniel Webster, representing the executors of Captain Foster's will, failed to sway the Court.

The legatees, without any legal redress, were obliged to content themselves with legacies much smaller than they had expected to receive. Examining this whole situation, and those who suffered because of it, we reach the rather strange conclusion that there was only one party to it who actually did not suffer at all.

And that person was Captain Israel Foster himself. As long as he lived there was plenty of money in the keg to meet his needs. There remained $13,000 at his death. As for the feeling of security which comes to any of us with the knowledge of a large sum of money in reserve, he enjoyed it as long as he lived, for he was quite unaware that the two culprits had made a hole in the bottom of the keg, abstracted the coins and filled the space with ballast iron.

So concludes the story of an event which hurt so many, excepting only Captain Foster; an episode which brings us today in close touch with life on this part of the Yankee coast in that early time and some of the significant events of its history.

$$18 \quad \text{\textit{~}}$$

Skipper Ireson's Ride

> Of all the rides since the birth of time,
> Told in story or sung in rhyme,
> The strangest ride that ever was sped,
> Was Ireson's, out from Marblehead.
> Old Floyd Ireson, for his hard heart,
> Tarred and feathered and carried in a cart,
> By the women of Marblehead.

Anyone who has read the poem which begins thus will be likely to conclude not only that it was "The strangest ride that ever was sped," but equally strange was the fact that it was written by John Greenleaf Whittier, New England's gentle and beloved Quaker poet. On a farm in Amesbury in the northern part of Essex County, Massachusetts, he lived an almost secluded life, rarely traveling far from his home.

Whittier's poems described nature, life in rural New England on the farm and the beaches. He wrote of Indians and witches, a two-headed snake and religion. Never a robust man, he was strong of mind and spirit, and his active intelligence was always ready for a new story, a new situation from which to create another poem.

249

So it came to pass that to John Greenleaf Whittier arrived the story of Skipper Ireson. It was strained and diluted and altered by the distance it had to travel, for in those days Marblehead was a long journey from Amesbury—a half a day's travel by various railroads. Today, of course, it is a scant hour's run in a motorcar.

Whittier saw here the makings of an epic ballad. It had everything appealing to the storyteller's heart: a wicked man whose act of inhumanity is punished by the spontaneous wrath of those whom he has injured, an unusual setting, picturesque characters, spectacular action, a grand climax. He gave this story everything he had—his skill as a poet, his dramatic capability, his deep background of culture.

And here is the way Whittier went about telling the story that had come to him in Amesbury from across the entire breadth of Essex County. Marblehead was a crowded and lusty town of rugged and outspoken seafaring folk, on a rocky peninsula jutting out into the stormy Atlantic on the southernmost reaches of Salem Bay. Whittier lived on a quiet farm in a rather secluded part of Amesbury, not far from the New Hampshire line. It was in this quietness that the Muse spoke and gave him *Skipper Ireson's Ride*.

The poem opens with the verse we have quoted. Then the poet passes to a description of the appearance of one who has been tarred and feathered, and there he must have drawn heavily on his imagination, for few have ever seen the victim of such an outrage.

> Body of turkey, head of owl,
> Wings a-droop like a rained on fowl,
> Feathered and ruffled in every part,
> Skipper Ireson stood in the cart.

Then the author proceeded to comment on the women of Marblehead, which was something in those days most safely done from a considerable distance.

> Scores of women, old and young,
> Strong of muscle, and glib of tongue,
> Pushed and pulled up the rocky lane,
> Shouting and singing the shrill refrain,
> Wrinkled scolds with hands on hips,
> Girls in bloom of cheek and lips,
> Wildeyed, free limbed, such as chase
> Bacchus round some antique vase,
> Brief of skirt, with ankles bare,
> Loose of kerchief and loose of hair.

Thus does the gentle Quaker poet describe the women of Marblehead in the year 1857. Anyone acquainted with the Marblehead of that time would be certain that had Whittier ventured into the town, these remarks would have earned him a tarring and feathering such as Ireson received, or perhaps the less complicated but more dangerous treatment of being "rocked around the corner."

Several stanzas of the poem describe Ireson's ride, his sorry appearance after being covered with tar and feathers and the women of Marblehead who, in a much stricter age than ours, were "free limbed, brief of skirt, with ankles bare," and "loose of kerchief and loose of hair." Then the reader arrives at the offense Ireson committed to earn this punishment.

> Small pity for him—he sailed away,
> From a leaking ship in Chaleur Bay.
> Sailed away from a sinking wreck,
> With his own town's people on her deck,
> "Lay by! lay by!" they called to him,
> Back he answered "Sink or swim,

> Brag of your catch of fish again"
> And off he sailed through the fog and rain.

There is his crime, one of the worst known to seafarers the world over. He refused to go to the rescue of mariners in distress, and for this any sailor would agree he had earned the hottest and most sulphurous spot in the Nether Pit. As if this were not bad enough, he had shown himself to be jealous of these shipwrecked fishermen because on some previous voyage they had come home with the best catch.

With a dark brush Whittier painted the results of Captain Ireson's crime in these words:

> Fathoms deep in dark Chaleur,
> That wreck shall lie forevermore,
> Mother and sister, wife and maid,
> Looked from the rocks of Marblehead,
> Over the moaning and rainy sea,
> Looked for the coming that might not be.

On through the town went the procession of townspeople meting out to Ireson his punishment here in this life. Again the poet, from distant Amesbury, dares thus to portray the ladies of Marblehead:

> Through the street, on either side,
> Up flew windows, doors swung wide,
> Sharp tongued spinsters, old wives gray,
> Treble lent the fish-horn's bray.

And the town's retired mariners, come ashore for good, are sketched in these lines.

> Sea-worn grandsires, cripple-bound,
> Hulks of old sailors run aground,
> Shook head and fist and hat and cane,
> And cracked with curses the hoarse refrain.

Whittier's lines take this mob scene through the town and out "along the Salem road," and there the poet's penchant for moralizing brings this violent ballad to a close with words of repentance from Skipper Ireson. He cries aloud to the mob:

Hear me, neighbors.

Presumably the uproar subsided sufficiently for him to continue:

What to me is this noisy ride?
What is the shame that clothes the skin,
To the nameless horror that lives within?
Waking or sleeping, I see a wreck,
And hear a cry from a reeling deck,
Hate me and curse me, I only dread,
The hand of God and the face of the dead.

Forgiveness then was the portion of Ireson who was "for his hard heart, tarred and feathered and carried in a cart, by the women of Marblehead." Absolution was expressed in these lines:

Then the wife of the skipper lost at sea,
Said "God has touched him. Why should we!"
Said an old wife mourning her only son,
"Cut the rogue's tether and let him run,"
So with soft relentings and rude excuse,
Half scorn, half pity, they cut him loose,
And gave him a cloak to hide him in,
And left him alone with his shame and sin.

So ends this masterpiece of the bard of old Essex County adding only the refrain:

Poor Floyd Ireson, for his hard heart,
Tarred and feathered and carried in a cart,
By the women of Marblehead.

This ballad was published in the *Atlantic Monthly* in 1857, and it was received with praise and acclaim by literate Americans everywhere. It added to the already considerable stature of the author as an American man of letters. In one place only was this work unappreciated—the town of Marblehead. One and all, the Marbleheaders were thoroughly insulted. They resented the liberties taken in representing the female half of the population, and they were annoyed at having attention called to an episode not creditable in any aspect.

Fortunately John Greenleaf Whittier had no occasion to visit Marblehead, so there occurred no similar affair with a poet this time, instead of a sea captain getting the treatment. Years passed, and the ire of the townspeople died down, but it was not extinguished. That the sense of insult had continued to smolder became evident in 1881 when the *History of Marblehead,* by Samuel Roads, was published.

Mr. Roads went to some pains to record the true facts of Skipper Ireson's ride. On October 30, 1808, the schooner *Betty,* whose master was Benjamin Ireson, not "old Floyd Ireson," arrived in Marblehead from the Grand Banks with a full fare of fish beneath her hatches. The crew told the story around town that off Cape Cod lighthouse they passed the schooner *Active* of Portland in a sinking condition, flying distress signals.

The crew said they besought Captain Ireson to come to and rescue these mariners. This Ireson refused to do, continuing on his course for his home port. Immediately this news got about town, Marblehead volunteers manned two schooners and sailed for the scene of the wreck but found nothing.

Upon their return to Marblehead, the two rescue vessels

found that the sloop *Swallow* had arrived with the master of the lost *Active* aboard. He reported that he had spoken Ireson's *Betty*, which continued on its course without giving any assistance. Soon after a whaleboat manned by Cape Codders came out from shore, took off four of *Active*'s crew, brought them ashore, and then returned for the other four.

However, the storm by this time had increased so much the whaleboat was not able to come alongside, the *Active* broke up, and the four men were lost. When this news reached Marblehead, the townspeople, well known as folks who favored direct and immediate action in any situation, proceeded to lay violent hands on Benjamin Ireson. Under the kettle a fire blazed, and they gave him a liberal application of tar as soon as it was warm enough to run. Then they commandeered someone's feather bed, slit it open and covered Ireson until he looked like some strange bird.

They appropriated someone's dory and put Captain Ireson in it. A couple of dozen men then laid hold of its painter and off they went, shouting and singing and roaring Marblehead language, which has a variety and vitality unknown anywhere else. They headed for adjoining Salem, a place for which no real Marbleheader had any use whatsoever, except as a spot in which to dump an undesirable, such as a sea captain who refused to come about to rescue mariners in distress.

The bottom came out of the dory, so they seized a cart from someone's premises, tossed their victim into it and continued. This is the stage of the journey Whittier heard about—the ride in the cart. The dory he does not mention, perhaps because the word "cart" lends itself to rhyming better than the word "dory."

The affair ended at the Salem line, where the Forest River

separates rough-and-ready Marblehead from its more prosperous and dignified neighbor. Word of the uproar had gone
ahead, and the Salem people had no intention of permitting a
mob of Marbleheaders to enter town, so the police and sailors,
armed with belaying pins and capstan bars, were ready to defend their border. Here the procession broke up, everyone returning to Marblehead with Ireson in his coat of tar and
feathers. Throughout his purgatory he had said nothing, but
when they let him go at his own house, he commented, "I
thank you for my ride, but you will live to regret it."

This is the account Roads gives of Ireson's ride. He goes on
to explain the skipper's parting remark by stating in his history that it appeared later it was the decision of the crew and
not the captain to stay on course, leaving the *Active*'s crew to
their fate. It was Captain Ireson who proposed to lay to until
the gale abated and then rescue the men, according to Roads,
and it was the crew who insisted on proceeding to Marblehead. Once in port, they made up the story of Ireson's refusal
and circulated it around town, with the result that the townspeople, incensed at the skipper's violation of this great law
of the sea, tarred and feathered him and took him on the ride
that has lived in history. Furthermore, said Roads, the women
did not participate.

In conclusion, Roads stated: "The fair name of the women
of Marblehead has been sullied by the fictitious story of one
of our best New England poets. It is but just that the true
history of the affair should be written."

When Whittier read this, twenty-three years after he had
written the ballad, he took pen in hand to write to Sam Roads.
"My verse was founded solely on a fragment of rhyme which I
heard from one of my early schoolmates, a native of Marble-

head," he wrote. "I supposed the story to which it referred dated back at least a century. I knew nothing of the participators and the narrative of the ballad was pure fancy.

"I am glad for the sake of truth and justice that the real facts are given in thy book. I certainly would not knowingly do injustice to anyone, dead or living."

So with a gentle bow Whittier, now living at Oak Knoll in Danvers, graciously made amends to Mr. Roads. We who know the Yankee coast have a few further thoughts on this subject.

To begin with, no one familiar with Marblehead ever heard anything resembling the dialect that Whittier, with the help of Editor Lowell of the *Atlantic Monthly,* put in the mouths of these fisherfolk. Furthermore, the resentment of Mr. Roads stemmed to a degree from the liberties Whittier took in describing the women of Marblehead. To his Victorian mind, it was insulting to suggest that the women would even be present at such an affair, much less take charge of it. So he said, "The fair name of the women of Marblehead has been sullied by the fictitious story." Perhaps Roads is right in suggesting that the women were not there, yet the tradition in some families has it that Great-grandmother was in the tumult that went roaring over the Salem road.

In his eagerness to exonerate Captain Ireson, Roads actually managed to put Marblehead in a worse position than that in which the poet placed it. If Ireson was not to blame, then eight Marbleheaders were guilty of this crime against the finest tradition of the sea. They refused to help fellow mariners in distress, these eight reprobates in Ireson's crew. Why, then, were they not tarred and feathered when the truth became known? They should at least have been "rocked around the corner." But it is hard to believe Marbleheaders would turn away from sailors in distress.

Furthermore, if they did not obey Captain Ireson's orders, they were guilty of the crime of mutiny. He should have gone to Boston and had them all indicted by a Federal Grand Jury. One other fact Roads overlooked. Ireson was not a Marbleheader; he came from Lynn. In the eyes of Marbleheaders he was a "foreigner," one who originated in outer darkness. It does not seem that Roads, a Marbleheader, had he known this, would have gone to such trouble to defend Ireson's reputation at the expense of representing his Marblehead crew members as being so low in the scale of life as to refuse to aid shipwrecked mariners, while Ireson, the "foreigner" from Lynn, had favored helping those aboard the sinking vessel.

It may be that Ireson did not bring mutiny charges for the reason that he had seen enough of the Federal Court in other matters. He had been hailed before that tribunal not long before on the charge of violating the Embargo Act of Congress which forbade Americans engaging in foreign commerce. His brigantine *William* in Lynn harbor transhipped freight to the *Mary* to be carried to a foreign port. As a result the *William* was confiscated by the Federal Government for violation of the Embargo Act.

However, the controversy over the accuracy of the poem has died down while poem itself remains. Vivid, dramatic, colorful, with a drumbeat such as few moderns can get into their verses, *Skipper Ireson's Ride* remains as a landmark in American literature, one of the best in the large volume the beloved bard of Essex County has left us. It is well worth a reading, and he who reads it will be sure to turn back to it again and again for its action and the music of its lines.

Bibliography

Allen, Gardner W. *Our Navy and the Barbary Corsairs*. Boston: Houghton Mifflin, 1905.

Bentley, Rev. William. *Diary of William Bentley (1784–1819)*. Salem: Essex Institute, 1905.

Callahan, North. *Henry Knox*. New York: Rinehart & Co., 1958.

Elkins, Leon Whitney. *Story of Maine: Coastal Maine*. Bangor: Hillsborough Co., 1924.

Felt, Joseph B. *Annals of Salem*, 2nd ed. Salem: W. & S. B. Ives, 1845.

French, Allen. *The Day of Concord and Lexington*. Boston: Little Brown, 1925.

French, Allen. *Siege of Boston*. New York: Macmillan, 1911.

Frothingham, Richard Jr. *History of the Siege of Boston and of the Battles of Lexington, Concord and Bunker Hill*. Boston: Charles C. Little and James Brown, 1849.

Maclay, Edgar Stanton. *History of American Privateers*. New York: D. Appleton & Co., 1899.

Morison, Samuel Eliot. *Maritime History of Massachusetts, 1783–1860*. Boston: Houghton Mifflin, 1921.

Naval Monument, Containing Official and Other Accounts of All the Battles Fought Between the Navies of the United States and Great Britain During the Late War; and an Account of the War with Algiers. Boston: A. Bowen, 1816.

259

Paine, Ralph D. *Ships and Sailors of Old Salem*. New York: Outing Publishing Co., 1908.

Peabody, Robert E. *Merchant Venturers of Old Salem*. Boston: Houghton Mifflin, 1912.

Phillips, James Duncan. *Pepper and Pirates: Adventures in the Sumatra Pepper Trade of Salem*. Boston: Houghton Mifflin, 1949.

Pickard, Samuel Thomas. *Life and Letters of John Greenleaf Whittier*. Boston: Houghton Mifflin, 1894.

Porter, Capt. David. *Journal of a Cruise Made to the Pacific Ocean in the United States Frigate Essex in the Years 1812, 1813, and 1814.*, 2nd ed. New York: Wiley & Halsted, 1822.

Roads, Samuel, Jr. *The History and Traditions of Marblehead*. Marblehead: N. Allen Lindsey & Co., 1897.

Sanderson, Carrie May. *Lynn in the Revolution, Compiled from Notes Gathered by Howard Kendall Sanderson*. Boston: W. B. Clarke, 1909.

U.S. Navy, Office of Naval Records and Library. *Naval Documents Related to the Quasi-War Between the United States and France*. Washington: Government Printing Office, 1938.

U.S. Navy, Office of Naval Records and Library. *Naval Documents Related to the United States Wars with the Barbary Powers*. Washington: Government Printing Office, 1939.

Wilson, Fred A. *Some Annals of Nahant, Massachusetts*. Boston: Old Corner Book Store, 1928.

Winsor, Justin. *Memorial History of Boston, 1630–1880*. Boston: Ticknor & Co., 1881.

The following articles from the Historical Collections of the Essex Institute, Salem, Massachusetts.

"The Affair at the North Bridge." Vol. 38, No. 4.

Endicott, G. M. "Leslie's Retreat." Proceedings, No. 13.

McKey, Richard H., Jr. "Elias Hasket Derby and the Founding of the Eastern Trade." Vol. 98, No. 1 and 2.

Smith, Philip C. F. "Crystal Blocks of Yankee Coldness." Vol. 97, No. 3.

Salem Gazette and *Salem Register,* Essex Institute Library, Salem, Mass.

Log Book of the Ship Mount Vernon. Peabody Museum, Salem, Mass.

"Mr. Tudor's Letter on the Ice Trade." Proceedings of the Massachusetts Historical Society, Vol. 3.

Index

263